Toxic Relationships

A comprehensive guide to understanding emotional manipulation in your relationships so you can stop feeling drained, isolated, and powerless and break free from the toxicity.

June Brockman

Table of Contents

Trigger warning: This book contains discussions on toxic relationships and abusive behaviors that might be upsetting for some readers.

Introduction

The worst part about toxic relationships is, you might not realize the toxicity as long as the relationship lasts. —Anand Thakur

Welcome to a journey of profound transformation on a path paved with the wisdom to recognize, heal, and rise above toxic relationships. This book is more than just a collection of pages; it's a sanctuary for those entangled in the invisible chains of emotional turmoil and a beacon of hope for those standing by, eager to lend support.

Our exploration begins by peeling back the layers of toxic relationships. These are connections that drain you, leaving behind a trail of self-doubt and emotional exhaustion. Here, you'll learn to spot the subtle yet unmistakable signs of toxicity; namely, the emotional manipulations and the insidious patterns of abuse that often go unnoticed.

At the heart of this book is your journey of healing and empowerment. It's about rediscovering your self-worth that may have been shadowed by negativity. We'll walk you through rebuilding the broken walls of self-esteem, erecting new boundaries forged from respect and self-care, and seeking the support that nurtures your soul back to wholeness.

Emerging stronger from the past, you'll learn how to safeguard your future. This book empowers you with the wisdom to discern and deter toxic dynamics, guiding you to forge relationships that are nurturing and fulfilling; relationships where respect and understanding flourish.

But this journey isn't just about personal transformation; it's also about extending your hand to others who are lost in this labyrinth. You'll find insights on how to build a compassionate community, offer resources and support, and become an anchor for those adrift in tumultuous emotional seas.

We want to paint a vision of a future brimming with hope and health. A future where your growth and well-being continue to bloom, nurtured by empowering relationships and a supportive community. This book is not just an ending but a beginning, a gateway to a life where every day is a step towards a brighter, more joyous existence.

In a world often shadowed by the weight of toxic dynamics, this book stands as a testament to the resilience of the human spirit and the boundless potential for renewal and happiness. It is an invitation to turn the page, to step into a narrative where you are the author of your own story, a story of triumph, healing, and everlasting growth. Let's embark on this journey together towards a horizon filled with promise and newfound strength.

Section 1:

Understanding Toxic Relationships

Chapter 1:

Unmasking Toxic Relationships

The moment you start to wonder if you deserve better, you do.
—Chenell Parker

The journey into understanding toxic relationships often begins with personal stories that echo universal truths. Sarah's experience with Mark, which started at a summer art festival, is one such story. Their connection was instant and intense, but as we will see, the initial charm and passion masked a gradual descent into toxicity. As we unravel the layers of Sarah's story, we'll explore the defining characteristics of toxic relationships, offering insights that may resonate with many.

In those early days, the relationship was engulfed in passion. Mark's affections were grand, his love declarations deep and frequent. However, as time unfolded, the initial bliss began to fade, revealing a more troubling reality beneath.

The shift in Mark's behavior was gradual. It began with small things: a sarcastic remark here, a slight put down there. These instances slowly morphed into a growing need for control, subtly infiltrating their daily life.

Initially, Sarah attributed these changes to the natural stresses of a new relationship. Her belief in love's power to conquer all led her to adopt a supportive stance, yet the more she agreed, the more demanding Mark became.

Mark's desire for admiration and attention grew increasingly clear. Conversations often revolved around him, overshadowing Sarah's own achievements. Her promotion at work, once a cause for mutual celebration, now received only tepid acknowledgment. Her stories and experiences were frequently interrupted or dismissed.

This dismissive attitude soon extended beyond words. Mark began to dictate their social engagements, even influencing Sarah's wardrobe choices. Every decision she made seemed to require his approval, signaling a shift in the power dynamics of their relationship.

The change in Sarah was not confined to her relationship; it permeated her very essence. Once vibrant and independent, she now wrestled with self-doubt and uncertainty. This erosion of her self-esteem was not abrupt but gradual, leaving her questioning her value and worth.

Joy and affection in their relationship grew scarce, overshadowed by an increasing sense of tension and unease. The relationship, once a haven, now felt more like a trap—a cycle of emotional upheaval that left her feeling drained and lost.

Mark's skill in emotional manipulation was subtle, yet effective. He had a knack for twisting situations to his advantage, often leaving Sarah feeling responsible for issues not of her making. Attempts to address problems were met with deflection, painting Mark as the victim and Sarah as the perpetrator.

Sarah's sense of isolation extended beyond the physical; it was emotional too. She felt increasingly cut off from her support network, hesitant to share her struggles for fear of judgment. Mark had become her world, a world where her needs and feelings were increasingly sidelined. Attempts to reach out to others were met with disapproval from Mark, further deepening her feelings of dependency.

Reflecting on her relationship, Sarah could see the patterns that had emerged: Mark's escalating control, the diminishing of her own desires, and the relentless emotional rollercoaster. This constant state of vigilance, attempting to avoid conflict and yet feeling powerless to instigate change, was exhausting.

Coming to terms with the reality of being in a toxic relationship was a painful but necessary awakening for Sarah. It forced her to reevaluate her understanding of love and partnership and confront the painful truth about her relationship with Mark.

Sarah's journey of unmasking the toxic nature of her relationship with Mark is not just her story—it's a reflection of the experiences of many who find themselves entangled in the subtle web of emotional manipulation. It's a narrative that resonates with the hidden struggles and silent battles fought behind the closed doors of seemingly perfect relationships.

Defining Toxic Relationships

As we explore toxic relationships, it becomes clear that Sarah's experiences are not isolated incidents. The issue they point out is common in different relationships. Understanding the complete extent of a toxic relationship requires exploring its defining characteristics and recurring patterns.

Recognizing Toxic Patterns

Emerging from Sarah's personal narrative, we find a universal theme: The insidious nature of toxic relationships. This understanding is crucial for anyone navigating similar circumstances. By defining what makes a relationship toxic, we can begin to unravel the complex web of behaviors and patterns that characterize such interactions.

In the landscape of toxic relationships, harmful behaviors are both the undercurrent and the storm. These behaviors, often subtle at the outset, grow progressively more damaging, eroding emotional well-being and distorting the victim's sense of reality.

At the heart of many toxic relationships lies emotional manipulation. This can manifest in various forms, such as gaslighting, where victims find themselves questioning their memory and perception, or through tactics like guilt-tripping and constant criticism. These methods serve not only to undermine the victim's self-esteem but also to fortify the manipulator's control.

Isolation is another insidious strategy, gradually implemented to increase the victim's dependency. It often begins innocuously, perhaps with the toxic partner expressing mild disdain for the victim's friends or family. Over time, this disdain can escalate, leading to a significant reduction in the victim's social interactions, further entrenching their dependency on the toxic partner.

Control in toxic relationships takes various guises. It may start with seemingly minor demands or preferences regarding the victim's choices, such as clothing or social activities. However, it can extend to more overt control, including financial domination, where the victim's financial freedoms are severely restricted.

The verbal and psychological abuse common in toxic relationships is particularly damaging. This abuse can range from derogatory comments and name-calling to more subtle forms of intimidation and humiliation. Unlike physical abuse, which leaves visible scars, the wounds inflicted by verbal and psychological abuse are often hidden, yet they run deep, causing lasting emotional trauma.

Physical violence, unfortunately, can also feature in the escalation of toxic relationships. What may begin as minor altercations can escalate into more severe and dangerous forms of physical abuse, posing a direct threat to the victim's physical safety.

Jealousy and possessiveness, often initially mistaken for signs of love and affection, can quickly morph into oppressive behaviors. Unwarranted accusations and efforts to control the victim's interactions with others are common manifestations of this toxic dynamic.

Stonewalling, the act of refusing to engage or communicate, serves to shut down any potential for healthy dialogue or resolution. This leaves the victim feeling ignored and invalidated, exacerbating the sense of loneliness.

Withholding affection is yet another tool in the arsenal of a toxic partner. This tactic involves using love and intimacy as means of control or punishment, leading the victim to feel unloved and unworthy.

Exploitation of the victim's emotions, where the abuser uses the victim's fears and vulnerabilities against them, is a common feature. This often results in the victim feeling responsible for the abuser's emotional state, fostering a toxic cycle of guilt and obligation.

Finally, the cycle of abusive behavior followed by apologies and promises of change is a hallmark of toxic relationships. This cycle creates a disorienting environment for the victim, filled with confusion and false hope.

Identifying these patterns is vital in recognizing and addressing toxic relationships. They are not just behaviors but signals of an underlying unhealthy dynamic, warning of potential harm and the need for intervention or change.

The emotional toll of being in a toxic relationship, as Sarah experienced, can be profound. Victims often suffer from long-term effects on their mental health, including decreased self-esteem, chronic anxiety, and a pervasive sense of worthlessness. These emotional scars can linger long after the relationship has ended, impacting future relationships and personal well-being. Sarah's diminishing confidence and increasing self-doubt reflect this deeper emotional impact, a common aftermath for many who find themselves in similar situations.

Understanding Manipulation and Control in Toxic Relationships

Manipulation and control, while distinct in their mechanisms, jointly create an environment of oppression and subjugation within a relationship. Manipulation operates on a more covert level, subtly influencing the victim's thoughts and actions without their clear awareness. Control, on the other hand, is more overt, directly imposing restrictions and commands on the victim.

In toxic relationships, emotional manipulation often takes forms that are subtle yet deeply impactful. For instance, Mark's constant criticism of Sarah, once disguised as playful teasing, evolved into blatant belittling of her achievements. He would often dismiss her opinions and emotions, subtly planting seeds of self-doubt in her mind. This pattern of undermining and invalidating is a classic example of emotional manipulation, where control is exerted not through overt actions but through eroding self-esteem.

Manipulators also use emotional leverage, such as guilt or sympathy, to bend the will of their partners to their desires. This form of manipulation is insidious because it's often veiled under the guise of care or concern, making it harder for the victim to recognize and confront.

Control, however, is more blatant. It may involve dictating how the victim spends their time, dresses, or interacts with others. Financial control is also common, where the abuser restricts the victim's access to money, effectively limiting their autonomy and freedom. Unlike manipulation, which can be elusive and hard to pinpoint, control often manifests in clear, discernible actions and demands.

Both manipulation and control serve to undermine the victim's independence and self-esteem. While manipulation confuses and disorients, control intimidates and restricts. Victims may find themselves constantly second-guessing their decisions, feeling as though they are living under a microscope, scrutinized and judged at every turn.

As seen in Sarah's story, control in toxic relationships can show up in different ways, like dictating social engagements and clothing choices. It often starts with small demands and escalates to complete domination over personal choices and freedoms.

Understanding the distinction between these two tactics is crucial in identifying toxic relationships. Recognizing manipulation requires a keen awareness of the subtler shifts in behavior and communication, while identifying control involves acknowledging the more explicit restrictions and impositions placed on the victim.

As we continue to explore these dynamics, it becomes evident that both manipulation and control are tools used to maintain power and dominance in a relationship. They are the mechanisms through which abusers instill fear, dependency, and a sense of helplessness in their victims, perpetuating the cycle of toxicity.

Differentiating Unhealthy Conflict from Normal Disagreements in Toxic Relationships

It's imperative to distinguish between unhealthy conflict, which is a hallmark of toxicity, and the normal disagreements that occur in any relationship. This distinction lies at the heart of identifying whether a relationship is harmful or healthy.

In toxic relationships, there is a persistent pattern of destructive interactions that define unhealthy conflict. These conflicts often escalate quickly, involve personal attacks, and lack any constructive resolution. In such scenarios, communication breaks down, respect is absent, and the primary goal seems to be winning the argument rather than understanding each other's perspectives. These conflicts leave deep emotional scars, as they are based on power dynamics and control, rather than mutual respect and problem-solving.

In contrast, normal disagreements, while potentially uncomfortable, are a natural part of any relationship. They stem from differences in opinions, preferences, or perspectives. How they are handled is what sets them apart. In healthy relationships, disagreements are approached with open communication and respect. Both parties are willing to listen, acknowledge each other's points of view, and work towards a mutually satisfactory resolution. These disagreements, rather than causing lasting harm, often lead to deeper understanding and growth in the relationship.

Sarah's experiences with Mark exemplify an unhealthy conflict. Their arguments were not about reaching an understanding, but about Mark asserting his dominance and belittling Sarah's opinions. Instead of constructive dialogue, there were patterns of verbal abuse, manipulation, and blame-shifting. This consistent negative pattern of conflict left Sarah feeling demeaned and powerless, a common outcome in toxic relationships.

The key to differentiating these two lies in the intent and outcome of the interactions. In healthy relationships, the intent is to resolve differences and strengthen the bond. In toxic relationships, the intent often revolves around control, domination, and diminishing the other person. The outcome in healthy relationships is mutual understanding and respect, whereas in toxic relationships, it is emotional damage and a further imbalance of power.

This understanding is crucial for anyone assessing the dynamics of their relationship. Recognizing the nature of conflicts and disagreements can be a significant indicator of whether a relationship is supportive and healthy or toxic and damaging.

Types of Toxic Relationships

We can't confine toxic relationships to romantic partnerships; they can manifest in various ways, influencing different parts of our lives. Understanding the spectrum of toxic relationships helps in recognizing and addressing them across different contexts.

1. **Romantic Relationships**: Often the most recognized form, toxic romantic relationships are marked by patterns of emotional manipulation, control, and abuse. These relationships can deeply impact an individual's emotional well-being and self-esteem.

2. **Family Relationships**: Toxic dynamics within families can be particularly challenging because of the inherent emotional bonds and expectations. This toxicity can manifest in various ways, from overbearing parents to sibling rivalries filled with continuous conflict and competition.

3. **Parent-Child Relationships**: These relationships can become toxic when there's excessive control, emotional manipulation, or neglect. The long-term impact on children can be profound, affecting their development and future relationships.

4. **Friendships**: Toxic friendships are characterized by a lack of support, one-sidedness, manipulation, and frequent conflicts. Such friendships drain energy and often lead to feelings of frustration and betrayal.

5. **Workplace Relationships**: Toxic dynamics in the workplace, whether with colleagues, superiors, or subordinates, can create a hostile and stressful environment. This toxicity can manifest as bullying, gossip, undue competition, or exploitation.

6. **Online and Virtual Relationships**: The digital age has introduced new arenas for toxic relationships, including online friendships or dating. These relationships may involve cyber-bullying, online harassment, or other forms of digital manipulation.

7. **Co-dependent Relationships**: In these dynamics, there's an excessive emotional or psychological reliance on each other, often to an unhealthy degree. It can lead to a lack of personal boundaries and hinder individual growth.

8. **Caretaker Relationships**: These can become toxic when one person predominantly acts as a caregiver, leading to feelings of resentment, exhaustion, and being underappreciated.

9. **Teacher-Student Relationships**: In educational settings, toxicity can arise in teacher-student interactions, characterized by favoritism, bullying, or abuse of power dynamics.

10. **Peer Relationships**: Among friends or acquaintances in various social settings, toxicity can manifest through bullying, exclusion, or manipulation.

The common thread in all these types of toxic relationships is the presence of harmful behaviors that undermine an individual's well-being, autonomy, and dignity.

Understanding the various forms of toxic relationships is the first step towards identifying and addressing them in our own lives. Recognizing these patterns empowers individuals to seek change, whether it's through setting boundaries, seeking support, or sometimes, ending the relationship.

The Gradual Nature of Toxicity in Relationships

Toxic relationships often start subtly, without clear signs of harm. Initially, these relationships can seem perfect, filled with positive experiences and emotional connections. However, over time, small yet harmful behaviors surface, marking the start of a gradual shift towards toxicity. These changes, such as a critical remark or an overreaction, can slowly become more frequent and severe, making it difficult to identify what's normal or acceptable.

The challenge in these relationships is the mix of positive moments with toxic behavior. This intermittent pattern of kindness, followed by harmful actions, creates confusion and false hope for improvement. The victim might make excuses for their partner's behavior.

As the relationship evolves, control and manipulation often become more pronounced. The partner's influence over decisions and actions grows, reducing the victim's independence and self-esteem. This increasing dominance is a clear sign of a toxic relationship.

Isolation is another gradual process in toxic relationships. It often starts with subtle suggestions to spend less time with friends or family and can grow into more direct efforts to cut off social contacts.

Parker's poignant observation, "The moment you start to wonder if you deserve better, you do," underscores the importance of trusting one's instincts when relationship dynamics feel unhealthy. Early recognition of these signs is key to addressing the issues and seeking change.

In Chapter 2, we'll explore specific indicators of harmful relationships. This chapter is crucial for understanding what to look out for and making informed decisions about your relationships. It's about equipping you with the knowledge to spot these warning signs and take steps towards healthier, more positive relationships.

The shift from understanding gradual toxicity to recognizing early signs is a crucial step. It's about moving from a general awareness of harmful patterns to identifying specific behaviors that show a relationship might be toxic. This awareness is the first step towards empowerment, self-respect, and healthier relationships.

Chapter 2:

Signs and Red Flags

A bad relationship can do that, can make you doubt everything good you
ever felt about yourself. —Husein Nishah

In exploring the labyrinth of toxic relationships, this chapter aims to unveil the signs and red flags that often remain hidden in plain sight. Through the lens of Sarah's evolving story with Mark, we will dissect the subtle nuances and overt warnings of toxicity.

Sarah's journey began with a whirlwind romance, filled with the intensity and passion that many dream of. Mark, with his charm and attentiveness, seemed to be the ideal partner. However, as their relationship progressed from those early days of infatuation to the realities of marriage, the façade began to crumble, revealing a more disturbing picture.

The initial grand gestures of love slowly gave way to patterns of behavior that undermined Sarah's confidence and sense of self. Mark's overwhelming devotion, initially seen as a sign of deep affection, gradually morphed into a tool for emotional manipulation. His self-centeredness began overshadowing Sarah's needs and emotions, belittling her achievements and subtly undermining her self-esteem. It was a classic case of love-bombing followed by devaluation; a pattern frequently observed in toxic relationships.

Mark exhibited a chronic sense of entitlement, exploiting Sarah's generosity and expecting special treatment without consideration for her feelings. His inability to take responsibility for his actions, coupled with frequent blame-shifting, left Sarah burdened with guilt and confusion. These early indicators, often missed or rationalized away, are tell-tale signs of a relationship steeped in emotional manipulation and control.

As we delve deeper into this chapter, we'll explore these indicators in greater detail, dissecting the manipulative language, the isolating tactics, and the control mechanisms employed in toxic relationships. We'll also examine the crucial role of intuition in recognizing these dynamics.

By understanding these signs, we aim to empower you with the knowledge and tools to identify toxic dynamics in their relationships, paving the way for healthier interactions and emotional well-being.

Emotional Manipulation Indicators

In dissecting the fabric of toxic relationships, it's imperative to understand the intricacies of emotional manipulation. By comprehensively exploring its indicators, we aim to equip readers with the knowledge to identify and address these harmful patterns.

Manipulative Language and Gaslighting

The use of manipulative language and gaslighting stands out as a subtle yet profound method of exerting control and undermining a partner's sense of reality. This tactic involves a sophisticated manipulation of words and actions to create doubt and confusion, leading to a significant imbalance in the relationship's power dynamics.

Manipulative language operates on various levels, from seemingly benign comments to overtly hurtful remarks. It might manifest as statements that trivialize the partner's feelings or experiences, such as telling them they are overreacting or being too sensitive. These phrases, though seemingly innocuous, are designed to belittle the partner's emotions and experiences, gradually eroding their self-confidence and ability to trust their own judgments.

Gaslighting takes this a step further by not only dismissing the partner's feelings, but also distorting their perception of reality. It's a psychological tactic where one person, through a range of behaviors and statements, makes their partner question their sanity, memory, and perception of events. This could involve an outright denial of events that occurred, contradicting the partner's recollections, or shifting blame to the partner for the manipulator's actions. For example, if confronted about a hurtful comment or action, the manipulator might deny ever saying or doing such a thing, asserting that the partner is misremembering or fabricating the event.

In Sarah's experience with Mark, elements of manipulative language and gaslighting were evident. Mark's dismissive attitude towards her achievements and feelings, combined with his tendency to contradict her recollections, left Sarah feeling disoriented and questioning her worth and sanity. These tactics were not random or unintentional; they were deliberate efforts to maintain control and keep Sarah in a state of subservience and uncertainty.

Recognizing the signs of manipulative language and gaslighting is essential in identifying toxic relationships. It requires attentiveness to how conversations and interactions make one feel. Consistent feelings of confusion, self-doubt, and a sense that one's reality is constantly being questioned are key indicators. Acknowledging these signs is a crucial step in addressing the imbalance in the relationship and seeking a path towards a healthier, more respectful partnership.

Isolation and Alienation

Isolation and alienation are tactics frequently employed in toxic relationships, serving as tools for control and emotional manipulation. These strategies involve cutting off the partner from their support network, creating a sense of dependency and loneliness that can be profoundly damaging.

Isolation typically starts subtly. It may begin with offhand comments that sow seeds of doubt about friends or family members, suggesting they are not supportive or have negative intentions. Gradually, these comments can escalate into more direct discouragement or even outright demands to cut off contact. The partner may find themselves increasingly alone, their world narrowing until the manipulator becomes their primary, if not sole, source of emotional support and interaction. This isolation is not merely physical but deeply emotional, creating a feeling of being cut off from others, a sense that no one else understands or can be trusted.

Alienation, a closely related tactic, further exacerbates this sense of isolation. The partner is made to feel that their concerns, feelings, and experiences are unique to the relationship and cannot be understood or supported by outsiders. This leads to a self-imposed withdrawal from social circles, as the partner begins to believe that sharing their experiences with others is futile or might result in judgment or misunderstanding. As stated in the resources provided by the Center for Women and Families, isolation and alienation effectively erode the partner's sense of self and external support, making them more vulnerable to manipulation and control.

In Sarah's relationship with Mark, these tactics of isolation and alienation were clearly visible. Mark subtly began to undermine her relationships with friends and family, casting them in a negative light and suggesting they didn't have her best interests at heart. Over time, Sarah found herself withdrawing from these relationships, feeling increasingly disconnected and alone. This isolation made her more dependent on Mark, amplifying the power imbalance in their relationship.

Recognizing the signs of isolation and alienation is crucial to identifying toxic relationships. It requires a careful reflection on changes in one's social dynamics and feelings of connectedness. Feeling cut off from friends and family, a sense of loneliness even in the other's presence, and a belief that others cannot understand our experiences are key indicators. Acknowledging these signs is a vital step towards addressing the toxic dynamics and seeking support to rebuild those crucial support networks.

Love-Bombing and Devaluation in Toxic Relationships

Love-bombing and devaluation emerge as critical phases that manipulators use to establish and maintain control. These tactics create a confusing push-and-pull dynamic that can be emotionally destabilizing for the partner.

Love-Bombing: The Illusion of Affection

Love-bombing is an intense period of affection and attention at the beginning of a relationship or after a conflict. It's characterized by grand gestures, lavish praise, and the rapid escalation of emotional intimacy. The manipulator showers their partner with compliments, gifts, and declarations of love and devotion, creating an overwhelming sense of being cherished and valued. This stage is designed to quickly win over our affection and trust, setting the stage for a deep emotional connection.

However, love-bombing is not about genuine affection; it's a calculated move to gain psychological leverage. As explained by experts in the field, including those from the Center for Women and Families, love-bombing serves to create a powerful bond that makes the partner more emotionally dependent and easier to manipulate.

Devaluation: The Shift to Disregard

Following the intense period of love-bombing, there often comes a stark shift to devaluation. The same partner who was once the object of intense affection is now subjected to criticism, disdain, and neglect. Compliments turn into criticisms, affection turns into indifference or hostility, and the partner is left feeling confused, hurt, and desperate to regain the lost affection.

Devaluation serves multiple purposes in a toxic relationship. It keeps the partner off-balance, continually striving to please the manipulator and return to the love-bombing phase. This cycle creates a dependency on the manipulator for emotional validation and self-worth, as the partner believes that they must be at fault for the change in behavior.

Recognizing the Cycle

This cycle often starts with love-bombing, where the manipulator overwhelms their partner with affection and attention, creating a sense of deep emotional connection. The partner, enveloped in this intense affection, becomes emotionally dependent on the manipulator. This phase sets the foundation for the manipulator to exert control over the partner.

The shift to devaluation follows, where the manipulator withdraws affection and replace it with criticism, indifference, or even outright hostility. The partner, once cherished, now finds themselves continually striving to regain the manipulator's approval and affection. This phase is marked by feelings of confusion, low self-esteem, and a desperate need to restore the relationship to an earlier state.

Sometimes, the cycle includes a phase of re-idealization, where the manipulator temporarily reverts to affectionate behavior. This phase is often short-lived and serves to keep the partner hopeful and tied to the relationship. The unpredictability of this cycle—the oscillation between affection and devaluation—creates a confusing and emotionally exhausting environment for the partner.

Recognizing the Signs

Recognizing this cycle involves being mindful of the patterns and shifts in the relationship. Key indicators include:

- A rapid onset of intense affection and attention (love-bombing).

- A sudden and unexplained shift to criticism and neglect (devaluation).

- Periods of affectionate behavior interspersed with phases of emotional distance or abuse.

- Feelings of confusion, anxiety, and a sense that one must work continually to earn the manipulator's affection.

Reflecting on Sarah's relationship with Mark, we can identify this cycle. A phase where Mark became critical and distant followed the initial period of intense love and attention. Sarah continually tried to please Mark and regain the affection she once received. This cycle led to significant emotional distress as she grappled with the inconsistency and unpredictability of Mark's behavior.

Breaking the Cycle

Breaking free from the cycle of emotional manipulation requires recognition of these patterns and an understanding that they are not reflective of a healthy relationship. It often involves seeking support from friends, family, or professionals who can provide perspective and guidance.

For those in such a cycle, it's important to remember that the manipulative behaviors are not a reflection of their worth or the love they deserve. Recognizing the cycle is the first step toward seeking healthier relationships and emotional well-being.

Behavioral Warning Signs

Behavioral warning signs are often more overt than emotional manipulation tactics, yet they can be equally damaging. This section explores these signs, focusing on controlling behavior and financial exploitation.

Controlling Behavior

Controlling behavior in relationships can often be mistaken for concern or protectiveness, but in reality, it's a significant red flag. This behavior goes beyond caring involvement; it's about exerting power and dominance, often at the cost of the partner's independence and self-esteem.

In a toxic relationship, controlling behavior manifests in various, sometimes subtle, ways. It might start with what appears as attentiveness—showing interest in the partner's daily activities, friends, and choices. However, this attentiveness gradually morphs into something more restrictive. A partner might start dictating who their significant other can see, what they can wear, or even how they should think and feel. It's not just about being involved in their life; it's about taking over it.

Such control can extend to monitoring communication by checking messages, emails, and call logs. It reflects a lack of trust and respect, turning the relationship into a surveillance state rather than a partnership. It might feel as if there's a constant overseer, evaluating and criticizing every action and decision.

Financial control is another aspect of this behavior. It involves taking charge of the partner's finances, from how they spend their money to making major financial decisions without their consent. This form of control can leave the partner financially dependent, struggling to make independent decisions or plan for their future without the controlling partner's approval or involvement.

Recognizing these signs of controlling behavior is vital. It's about noticing a shift from mutual respect and support to a dynamic where one partner holds disproportionate power over the other. This shift can be insidious, making it challenging to identify until the control is firmly established.

Moving forward from such a dynamic requires courage and self-awareness. It might involve having tough conversations about boundaries and mutual respect. Sometimes, seeking external support from friends, family, or professionals can provide the perspective and strength to address these issues.

It's essential for individuals in such situations to understand that control is not synonymous with love or care. Healthy relationships are built on trust, mutual respect, and the freedom for each individual to be their own person. Breaking free from controlling behavior is a step towards reclaiming one's autonomy and finding a relationship dynamic that nurtures and respects both partners equally. Such behavior is not about caring or protection; it's about ownership and control.

Exploitation and Financial Manipulation

In the intricate dynamics of toxic relationships, exploitation and financial manipulation often emerge as significant yet insidious elements. These behaviors go beyond the normative give-and-take of a healthy relationship, morphing into a means of control and subjugation.

Exploitation in a relationship can take various forms. It often involves using the partner for one's personal gain, whether emotional, financial, or social. This could mean taking advantage of the partner's kindness, generosity, or love, without intending to reciprocate or acknowledge their efforts. It's a one-sided dynamic where the manipulator benefits at the expense of their partner's well-being.

Closely linked to exploitation is financial manipulation, a particularly damaging form of control. Financial manipulation involves exerting power over the partner's financial resources, making significant decisions without their consent, or restricting their access to funds. This control can manifest in many ways, from dictating how the partner spends their money to completely taking over their finances. In extreme cases, it might involve accruing debt in the partner's name or stealing their assets, leaving them financially vulnerable and dependent.

The impact of these behaviors on the partner can be profound. Financial manipulation, in particular, can lead to a loss of independence and a feeling of entrapment within the relationship. The partner may find themselves unable to make personal choices or plan for their future without the manipulator's involvement or approval. This loss of financial autonomy is not just a matter of money; it's a significant blow to the partner's sense of self and agency.

Identifying exploitation and financial manipulation requires an awareness of the balance of power and reciprocity in the relationship. It's about recognizing when one's generosity or resources are being used without fair return or respect. It involves being mindful of how financial decisions are made and who benefits from them.

Addressing these issues is a crucial step towards establishing a healthier relationship dynamic. It may involve setting clear boundaries around finances, seeking legal or financial advice, or in some cases, reevaluating the future of the relationship. For those experiencing financial manipulation, it's important to remember that support is available, and steps can be taken to regain financial independence and control.

Ultimately, moving away from exploitation and financial manipulation is about reestablishing respect and equality in the relationship. It's a journey towards ensuring that both partners' needs, contributions, and aspirations are valued and supported equally.

Identifying Behavioral Warning Signs and Moving Forward

In the landscape of toxic relationships, recognizing behavioral warning signs is crucial for understanding and addressing the unhealthy dynamics that may be at play. These signs, often more overt than emotional manipulations, can serve as clear indicators of the relationship's true nature.

Behavioral warning signs in a toxic relationship often manifest as a feeling of being monitored or restricted in one's activities and decisions. This control can range from more intrusive or invasive behaviors, such as a partner excessively questioning your whereabouts and dictating your social interactions, to more covert or subtle behaviors, such as a partner subtly or implicitly prompting you to do their bidding in any given circumstance through tailored manipulation.

These behaviors are not hallmarks of a caring and supportive relationship, but indications of control and manipulation. In a healthy relationship, partners respect each other's autonomy and privacy. They make decisions together, valuing mutual consent and understanding. Financial independence is respected, and there is a balance of give and take that supports each partner's individuality and growth.

Identifying these signs requires a keen awareness of how the relationship's dynamics have evolved. A shift from mutual respect and support to control and restriction is a significant indicator that the relationship may veer into unhealthy territory. It's important to trust one's instincts and observations in these situations, acknowledging any feelings of discomfort or unease about how the relationship is progressing.

Acknowledging these behavioral warning signs is the first step toward addressing the underlying issues. This process may involve setting boundaries to safeguard one's autonomy and well-being. Seeking support from friends, family, or professionals can provide valuable perspectives and guidance on how to navigate these challenges. Sometimes, it might become necessary to consider leaving the relationship, especially if attempts to resolve these issues don't lead to meaningful change.

Moving forward from a toxic relationship requires courage and self-compassion. It's important for individuals to know that help is available and that they deserve a relationship based on mutual respect and equality. This journey might involve personal reflection, professional counseling, and rebuilding one's sense of self outside the confines of the controlling dynamics.

In taking these steps, individuals can find their way towards healthier, more fulfilling relationships, where their autonomy, individuality, and emotional well-being are respected and nurtured.

Gut Instinct and Intuition

These innate instincts, though intangible and hard to quantify, can serve as powerful indicators, alerting us to underlying issues that might not be immediately visible.

Gut feelings arise from our subconscious, piecing together subtle cues and patterns that our conscious mind may overlook or rationalize away. In a toxic relationship, these feelings might manifest as a persistent sense of unease, discomfort, or anxiety, even when everything appears fine on the surface. It's that nagging sensation that something is off, even if you can't put your finger on exactly what it is.

For example, in a relationship where emotional manipulation or controlling behavior is present, you might feel constantly on edge, as if you're walking on eggshells. There could be moments where you feel overwhelmingly sad, confused, or drained without a logical reason. These feelings are your mind and body's way of signaling that the emotional environment around you might be harmful.

Trusting these gut feelings is an important step in acknowledging and addressing potential issues in a relationship. It involves giving credence to your emotions and perceptions, even when they seem to contradict the outward appearance of your relationship. It's about listening to that inner voice that whispers doubts and concerns, and not dismissing these feelings as mere overreactions or paranoia.

Acting on your intuition doesn't necessarily mean making immediate drastic changes, but it does call for a closer examination of your relationship. It might involve reflecting on how your partner's actions make you feel, considering the patterns of your interactions, or talking about your feelings with trusted friends or a professional for an outside perspective.

Many times, people who have moved away from toxic relationships reflect on how their gut feelings were early indicators of the issues they later faced. They often wish they had listened to and trusted these instincts sooner. These feelings are a natural, protective response, honed by our experiences and observations, and they can help to guide us toward healthier, more fulfilling relationships.

Recognizing and respecting your gut feelings is a step towards self-care and self-respect. It empowers you to take control of your emotional well-being and to seek relationships that are nurturing, respectful, and supportive.

Intuition vs. Paranoia

It's important to differentiate between intuition and paranoia. Intuition is a subtle, often unexplainable sense of knowing that something is wrong, based on picking up on real but subtle cues. Paranoia, on the other hand, is characterized by irrational fears and a tendency to misconstrue situations without a factual basis.

It's crucial to strike a balance between paying attention to intuitive feelings while ensuring these feelings are grounded in the reality of the relationship dynamics.

Moving Forward

Looking back, Sarah realized that her intuition had been signaling the toxicity in her relationship with Mark all along. There were moments when she felt belittled, controlled, or isolated, which her intuition recognized as warning signs. Acknowledging and trusting these feelings could have been a crucial step in addressing the issues earlier.

As we conclude this exploration, it's crucial to reflect on the insights gained and consider how they apply to our own relationships and those around us.

Reflecting on these topics, consider how they manifest in your own relationships. Are there patterns or behaviors that resonate with what you've learned? How might you respond differently now, armed with this knowledge?

Equipped with a deeper understanding of toxic dynamics, we are better prepared to recognize and address these issues, whether in our lives or in supporting others. As we move forward, it's important to remember that knowledge is a tool for empowerment. Recognizing the signs of a toxic relationship is the first step toward seeking change.

We will explore the specific characteristics of narcissism and manipulative personalities. Understanding these traits is essential for comprehending the deeper underlying factors that drive toxic behaviors in relationships.

Chapter 3:

Understanding Narcissism and Manipulative Personalities

Sometimes, we refuse to see how bad something is until it completely destroys us. —Dr. Anne Brown

This observation sets the stage as we delve into the complexities of narcissistic and manipulative personalities. Said personalities, often elusive in their manifestation, can have profound impacts not only on personal relationships but also in professional environments.

Take, for example, the case of Angie, a coworker whose narcissistic and manipulative traits became a significant challenge in her workplace. Angie's story is a typical example of how such personalities operate in real-world settings. On the surface, Angie was charismatic, easily winning over her colleagues with her apparent confidence and skill. However, beneath this facade lay a different reality, one marked by an exaggerated sense of self-importance and a relentless pursuit of personal gain at the expense of others.

Angie's interactions were laced with subtle manipulation. She had a talent for making others doubt their own judgments and worth, often taking credit for their ideas and achievements. Her grandiose tales of personal success were designed to undermine her peers, positioning herself as superior. Behind the scenes, Angie's manipulative nature played out through the spreading of gossip, pitting colleagues against each other, and skillfully shifting alliances to ensure she remained at the center of attention.

We will dissect the intricate layers of narcissistic and manipulative personalities like Angie's. We'll look closely at the defining traits of narcissism, understand the spectrum on which these traits can exist, and explore the various types of manipulative personalities. Additionally, we will delve into the dynamics of codependency and how it plays into relationships with narcissistic individuals.

The insights gleaned here will not only aid in recognizing such traits in others but also in understanding their impact on interpersonal and professional relationships.

The Narcissistic Personality: Defining Narcissism

Narcissistic Personality Disorder (NPD) stands as a formidable presence in the pantheon of psychological disorders, marked by a constellation of traits that profoundly impact both the individual and those in their relational orbit. At the heart of NPD lies a trio of defining characteristics: Grandiosity, a relentless need for admiration, and a notable lack of empathy. Let's take a look.

Grandiosity: The Hallmark of Narcissism

Grandiosity, the cornerstone trait of narcissism, manifests as an inflated sense of self-importance and superiority. Individuals with NPD often exhibit an exaggerated perception of their achievements and capabilities. This grandiose self-view is not merely an overinflated ego but a deep-seated conviction of being exceptional, unique, and deserving of special treatment.

This grandiosity is frequently expressed through boastful and pretentious behavior. The individual may engage in self-aggrandizing narratives, often exaggerating their accomplishments and talents. These stories, however, are not just braggadocio; they serve a psychological purpose. They prop up a fragile self-esteem that, paradoxically, lies beneath the surface of the narcissistic persona.

The Need for Admiration: A Narcissist's Fuel

Closely intertwined with grandiosity is the narcissist's insatiable need for admiration and validation. This craving for recognition and applause is not merely a desire but a necessity for maintaining their self-esteem and self-image. The narcissistic individual often seeks out positions of prominence and attention where they can be the center of admiration.

Their interactions are often calibrated to elicit praise and affirmation. This need can drive them to achieve impressive feats, yet the motivation is not purely for the accomplishment itself but for the accolades that follow. In personal relationships, this need for admiration can create a dynamic where the narcissist demands constant validation and approval from their partners, friends, and family.

Lack of Empathy: The Narcissist's Blind Spot

Perhaps the most detrimental aspect of NPD in the context of interpersonal relationships is the pronounced lack of empathy. Empathy, the ability to understand and share the feelings of another, is often underdeveloped or absent in individuals with narcissistic traits. This deficit affects their ability to form deep, meaningful connections with others.

The narcissist's lack of empathy manifests in several ways. They may be dismissive or indifferent to the feelings and needs of others, view relationships primarily through the lens of personal benefit, or be insensitive to the impact of their actions on others. This lack of empathy can lead to relationships characterized by superficiality, exploitation, and emotional neglect.

The Impact on Interpersonal Relationships

The interplay of these core traits—grandiosity, need for admiration, and lack of empathy—creates a relationship dynamic fraught with challenges. Narcissists often struggle to maintain healthy, long-term relationships. Their partners may initially be drawn to the narcissist's charisma and confidence but soon find themselves in a one-sided relationship where their needs and feelings are secondary.

In romantic relationships, the narcissist's partner often feels undervalued and emotionally neglected. The narcissist's inability to empathize and their constant need for admiration can lead to a cycle of emotional abuse and manipulation. Friendships and familial relationships are similarly impacted. The narcissist may leverage these relationships for their gain while offering little in return, leading to strained and often contentious dynamics.

In a professional context, individuals with NPD can be both charismatic leaders and difficult colleagues. Their drive for success may propel them to positions of power, but their lack of empathy and need for admiration can create toxic work environments marked by conflict, competition, and instability.

Understanding Narcissistic Personality Disorder is crucial in recognizing and addressing the challenges it presents in interpersonal relationships. While individuals with NPD can be charming and alluring, the underlying traits of grandiosity, need for admiration, and lack of empathy often lead to problematic and sometimes destructive relationship dynamics. Recognizing these traits is the first step in fostering healthier interactions and seeking appropriate support or intervention.

The Spectrum of Narcissism: A Varied Landscape of Self-Perception

Narcissism, often misconceived as a singular trait, actually spans a broad spectrum, ranging from healthy self-esteem to extreme pathological behaviors. This spectrum encapsulates the diverse ways narcissism manifests in individuals, influencing their behavior and the dynamics of their relationships.

At one end of this spectrum is what Telloian (2021) refers to as "healthy narcissism." It's the foundational block of a balanced self-image, where a person possesses a realistic sense of self-worth and confidence. This form of narcissism is vital for personal development, enabling individuals to pursue their ambitions while maintaining empathy and forming meaningful connections. Picture an entrepreneur whose self-assurance is the driving force behind their success, yet they remain grounded and considerate of others.

Progressing along this spectrum, we encounter adaptive narcissism. Here, narcissistic traits are present but in moderation. These individuals are characterized by their self-confidence and ambition, qualities that often lead to professional and personal achievements. Despite their high self-regard, they preserve the ability to empathize and engage in healthy relationships. Think of a corporate executive who ambitiously climbs the career ladder but still cherishes and nurtures their family life and friendships.

In the gray area of subclinical narcissism, the traits become more noticeable. Individuals within this category seek attention and validation more actively and may struggle with maintaining empathy. Their relationships often face some strain due to these elevated narcissistic tendencies, such as a local celebrity who thrives on public admiration but faces challenges in sustaining close, intimate relationships.

As we move towards the extreme end of the spectrum, we encounter Narcissistic Personality Disorder (NPD). Defined by Rogoza et al. (2018) as a pervasive pattern of grandiosity and a lack of empathy, NPD significantly disrupts interpersonal relationships. Individuals with NPD are prone to manipulative and exploitative behavior, often leading to emotionally turbulent and unstable relationships. Imagine a high-profile CEO whose relentless pursuit of power and admiration comes at the expense of genuine emotional connections, often leaving a trail of strained relationships.

At the darkest end of the spectrum lies malignant narcissism. This severe form combines the traits of NPD with antisocial behavior, often manifesting in aggressive, deceitful, and even harmful actions towards others. Malignant narcissists can inflict significant psychological and sometimes physical damage in their relationships. A political figure with a cruel streak and a blatant disregard for moral and ethical standards could exemplify this form of narcissism.

Understanding the narcissistic spectrum is essential not only for recognizing the various manifestations of narcissism but also for appreciating how these traits influence individual behavior and interpersonal dynamics. From the healthy self-regard of the entrepreneur to the destructive patterns of the malignant narcissist, the spectrum highlights the complexity and diversity of narcissistic traits.

Manipulative Personality Types: Covert and Overt Manipulators

Have you ever felt bewildered in a relationship, sensing hidden strings being pulled but unable to identify the puppeteer? Here, I aim to unveil the complexities of manipulative personalities. Understanding these personalities is crucial for recognizing and navigating the often-subtle dynamics of manipulation.

Overt Manipulators: The Bold and the Assertive

Overt manipulators stand out for their brazen and assertive methods. These individuals do not hide their intentions; instead, they wield their influence openly, often using power and dominance as their tools. This section explores various types of overt manipulators, from aggressors and bullies to gaslighters and blamers. Each type uses distinct tactics to assert control, creating dynamics that are as unmistakable as they are damaging. Understanding these personality types is crucial for recognizing and responding to overt manipulation in relationships.

- **Aggressors**: Aggressors are blatant in their use of threats and intimidation, resorting to fear-based manipulation to force compliance. Similarly, bullies target vulnerabilities, using relentless aggression to intimidate and control. Their actions often lead to a relationship atmosphere rife with tension and anxiety. Reflect on this: Have you ever felt overpowered by someone's direct aggression in a relationship?

- **Bullies**: Bullies are individuals who use power, whether physical, social, or emotional, to intimidate or harm others. They often seek to dominate or control their targets through aggressive behavior, which can include physical confrontation, verbal insults, social exclusion, or spreading rumors. Bullies may target individuals they perceive as vulnerable or different, attempting to assert their dominance or ease their own insecurities by demeaning others.

- **Gaslighters**: As described by Ducharme (2018), gaslighters manipulate by denying reality, making their targets question their memory and sanity. They use doubt as a tool to undermine others' confidence.

- **Blamers**: Blamers skillfully shift responsibility onto others, evading accountability. By playing the blame game, they twist situations to their advantage, often leaving their partners feeling responsible for issues that are not theirs to bear.

- **Seducers**: Seducers, with their charm and flattery, create an illusion of affection and interest. They often employ love-bombing, a tactic where overwhelming attention and affection are used to gain trust and control. Similarly, flatterers use excessive praise to manipulate, playing on vulnerabilities and insecurities.

- **Demanders**: They exert their influence by making unreasonable demands, often using guilt and pressure to manipulate compliance. Their relentless expectations can create a one-sided power dynamic in relationships.

- **Competitors**: These individuals turn relationships into constant competitions. By establishing a comparison-based dynamic, they seek to assert dominance and control, often leaving their partners feeling perpetually inadequate or undervalued.

- **Drama Queens/Kings**: Thriving in chaos, they manipulate by crafting dramatic scenarios. By drawing others into their turmoil, they seek attention and control, often at the emotional expense of those around them.

Covert Manipulators: The Subtle and the Deceptive

Contrasting with their overt counterparts, covert manipulators operate under a guise of subtlety and deception. Their tactics are not immediately apparent, cloaked in behaviors that may initially seem benign or even caring. This section delves into the world of covert manipulation, examining types such as victim players, silent treatment givers, passive-aggressors, and guilt-trippers. Their methods are insidiously effective, often leaving their targets in a state of confusion and self-doubt. Recognizing these subtle manipulators is a more challenging but equally vital step in protecting oneself from emotional manipulation.

1. **Victim players**: These manipulators portray themselves as perennial victims, eliciting sympathy and support to control others. They expertly deflect attention from their actions by invoking pity and compassion.

2. **Silent treatment givers**: By withholding communication and affection, these manipulators use emotional withdrawal as punishment and control. The silence can be as painful and disorienting as any verbal onslaught, leaving their partners in a state of confusion and distress.

3. **Passive-aggressors**: As highlighted by Sarkis (2022), passive-aggressors express their hostility indirectly. Through sarcasm, backhanded compliments, and subtle sabotage, they create an environment of hidden hostility, often leaving their partners second-guessing the true intent behind their words and actions.

4. **Guilt-trippers**: Masters of emotional manipulation, guilt-trippers create a sense of obligation and indebtedness. They skillfully use guilt to control the actions and decisions of others, often leaving their partners feeling perpetually beholden.

5. **Innocent personas**: These manipulators project an image of innocence or naivety to disarm suspicion. By exploiting perceived vulnerability, they manipulate others, often catching their partners off guard with their hidden agendas.

6. **Triangulators**: Involving third parties, triangulators manipulate relationship dynamics. They use these triangles to control and influence, creating conflicts and misunderstandings between people.

7. **Secret-keepers**: By withholding information and keeping secrets, they create an information imbalance. This selective disclosure is a tool for manipulation, often leaving their partners feeling out of the loop and disempowered.

8. **Flatterers**: They use excessive flattery and praise to ingratiate themselves with others, exploiting vulnerabilities and insecurities for manipulation.

Overt manipulators often create a dynamic of fear and compliance, leading to relationships marked by tension and conflict. Their aggressive and assertive tactics can result in emotional stress and a breakdown of trust.

Covert manipulators, on the other hand, create a more insidious impact. Their subtle manipulation tactics can lead to confusion, self-doubt, and emotional turmoil in their targets. The deceit and emotional manipulation involved in covert tactics often make it challenging for the targets to recognize the manipulation, leading to prolonged exposure to toxic dynamics.

Whether overt or covert, these personalities have a significant impact on interpersonal dynamics, often leading to emotional distress and dysfunction. Recognizing these traits and behaviors is the first step towards establishing boundaries and seeking healthier interactions.

Understanding Codependency: The Emotional Dynamics of Relational Dependency

Codependency often emerges in relationships where one individual finds their self-worth and identity predominantly through the act of caring for the other, who might be grappling with issues like addiction or mental health challenges. This condition manifests in various ways, creating an imbalance in the relationship that can have profound emotional consequences.

At the core of codependency is an excessive degree of caretaking. This is not just about looking after the well-being of another but doing so to an extent that eclipses one's own needs.

Consider the case of Jamie, who spent years prioritizing the needs of Alex, their alcoholic partner. Jamie's identity became so intertwined with Alex's struggles that Jamie's own aspirations and well-being were continually sidelined. This behavior is emblematic of codependency, where the caretaker derives their sense of value and purpose almost exclusively from their role in the other person's life.

These relationships are often marked by a significant lack of boundaries. Individuals like Jamie struggle to distinguish between helping and enabling, often dissolving into the emotional landscape of their partner. This blurring of lines is not limited to physical care but extends into the emotional realm. The emotional state of the codependent becomes wholly reactive to that of their partner, leading to a loss of personal emotional autonomy.

Low self-esteem underpins many of these dynamics. Codependents often grapple with feelings of unworthiness, seeking validation through their ability to be indispensable to someone else. This search for validation through others leads to a paradoxical situation: The more they sacrifice for their partner, the less they attend to their own self-care, further diminishing their sense of self-worth.

The emotional toll of codependency can lead to chronic unhappiness, given that the relationship rarely fulfills the emotional needs of the codependent. Stress and anxiety are common, as the codependent navigates the complex web of their partner's issues, often feeling solely responsible for managing these challenges. Over time, resentment builds as the imbalance in the relationship becomes increasingly apparent.

The journey of the codependent often involves a deep realization of these patterns and a conscious decision to seek change. This might mean setting healthier boundaries, seeking therapy, or sometimes, stepping away from the relationship. It is a path marked by the recognition that self-care is not selfish but essential, and that true love and support in a relationship should be mutual and not one-sided.

Codependency reflects a complex interplay of emotional dependency, low self-esteem, and blurred boundaries.

The Codependent-Narcissist Dynamic: A Complex Interplay of Emotional Dependency

The relationship between codependents and narcissists represents a particularly complex and often toxic dynamic. It's a dance of mutual dependency, where each partner plays a role that perpetuates and exacerbates the dysfunction in their relationship.

Formation of the Codependent-Narcissist Dynamic

This dynamic typically begins with an almost magnetic attraction. The narcissist, with their grandiose sense of self and need for admiration, finds a willing audience in the codependent, who thrives on being needed and is quick to cater to others' needs. Consider the relationship between Lisa, a codependent, and Jordan, a narcissist. Lisa was initially drawn to Jordan's confidence and charm, mistaking these traits for strength and security. For Jordan, Lisa's willingness to prioritize his needs above her own was a source of constant ego nourishment.

How the Dynamic Persists

In the codependent-narcissist relationship, there is an unspoken agreement: The codependent gets a sense of purpose and value by catering to the narcissist's needs, while the narcissist receives the admiration and validation they crave. However, this dynamic is fraught with emotional harm. The narcissist, often lacking empathy and preoccupied with their own desires, may exploit the codependent's willingness to please, leading to a cycle of emotional abuse and manipulation.

For instance, Jordan would regularly demean Lisa, questioning her intelligence and capabilities. Lisa, in her codependent role, would internalize these criticisms, believing she needed to try harder to please Jordan. This cycle reinforced Jordan's dominant position in the relationship, while Lisa's self-esteem and sense of self-worth continually eroded.

Impact on Both Parties

The impact of this dynamic on the codependent can be devastating. They often lose their sense of self, living in constant fear of failing to meet the narcissist's needs or expectations. This can lead to anxiety, depression, and a feeling of being trapped in an emotionally draining relationship.

For the narcissist, while the relationship superficially meets their needs for attention and validation, it prevents any real emotional growth or self-reflection. Narcissists remain stuck in their patterns of manipulation and control, often unaware of the emotional damage they are causing.

Addressing and Resolving the Dynamics

Breaking free from the codependent-narcissist dynamic requires significant effort and often professional intervention. For the codependent, this might involve therapy to build self-esteem, learn to set boundaries, and recognize their intrinsic value outside of their role as a caretaker. For the narcissist, therapy can help in developing empathy, recognizing the impact of their behavior on others, and learning healthier ways of relating to people.

In cases like Lisa and Jordan's, it may be necessary to end the relationship to allow both individuals to work on their issues separately. However, in situations where both parties are committed to change, couple's therapy can offer a pathway to transforming the relationship into a healthier, more balanced partnership.

The codependent-narcissist dynamic is a complex interplay that requires understanding, patience, and often professional help to resolve. Recognizing the signs of this dynamic is the first step towards change. For those caught in this cycle, there is hope in the possibility of healing and finding healthier ways of relating to others.

Navigating the Treacherous Waters of Codependency and Narcissism

In the tangled web of relationships, few dynamics are as complex and destructive as the interplay between a codependent and a narcissist. This dynamic, a dance of emotional extremes, often spirals into a cycle of toxicity and dysfunction. Angie's manipulative and narcissistic traits at the workplace, as introduced at the beginning of this chapter, offer a glimpse into this intricate dynamic.

Angie, with her grandiose sense of self and insatiable need for admiration, represents the quintessential narcissist. Her colleagues, drawn in by her charm, unwittingly play the role of the codependent. They continuously feed Angie's ego, despite her undermining and manipulative tactics. This dynamic, while set in a professional environment, mirrors the personal relationships where codependency and narcissism often intertwine.

The codependent-narcissist relationship typically starts with an intense attraction. They draw the codependent to through the unwavering confidence and magnetic allure, finding comfort in being indispensable. The codependent, often self-sacrificing and eager to please, provides the perfect audience for the narcissist's grandiosity. However, this seemingly symbiotic relationship soon reveals its toxic nature.

As the relationship progresses, the codependent becomes increasingly enmeshed in the narcissist's world. Their desire to be helpful is exploited by the narcissist, who perceives this as an opportunity to dominate and control. The codependent's self-worth becomes tied to their ability to appease the narcissist, leading to a cycle of self-sacrifice and neglect of their own needs.

For Angie's colleagues, this meant continuously walking on eggshells, always cautious not to bruise her ego while enduring her subtle yet persistent manipulations. They found themselves isolated, their own professional needs and aspirations sidelined in favor of Angie's whims.

The impact of this dynamic on both parties can be profound. The codependent, in their relentless pursuit to satisfy the narcissist, often loses their sense of identity and self-worth. They may experience anxiety, depression, and a feeling of being trapped in a relationship that drains rather than fulfills them. The narcissist, while benefiting from the relationship, remains emotionally stunted, their true potential for growth and empathy hindered by their incessant need for control and admiration.

Breaking free from this toxic cycle requires introspection, courage, and often professional help. For the codependent, this means learning to set boundaries, acknowledging their own worth independently of the narcissist, and seeking support to rebuild their self-esteem. For the narcissist, it requires a willingness to confront their own vulnerabilities, develop empathy, and engage in healthier ways of relating to others.

In the workplace, as in personal relationships, understanding and addressing the dynamics of codependency and narcissism can lead to healthier, more fulfilling interactions. For Angie's colleagues, recognizing the toxic patterns was the first step towards asserting their own professional boundaries and reclaiming their autonomy.

We need to understand that navigating narcissistic and manipulative personalities is both challenging and essential. Recognizing these traits and dynamics empowers individuals to make informed decisions, fostering healthier relationships and personal growth. Next, we will explore another facet of manipulation that often intersects with narcissism and codependency.

Chapter 4:

Gaslighting: When Reality Feels Like a Mirage

Don't light yourself on fire trying to brighten someone else's existence.
—Charlotte Eriksson

Lucas' journey began in a home where words were not just a means of communication but tools of a more insidious nature. From a young age, he learned that conversations with his mother were never straightforward. They were labyrinths in which his reality was constantly questioned and reshaped.

Lucas still vividly remembers his 10th birthday, a day that should have been filled with joy and celebration. Instead, it turned into a confusing ordeal. Excitedly recounting a story from school, he was suddenly interrupted by his mother's stern voice, "Lucas, that's not how it happened. You're remembering it wrong again." The room fell silent. Lucas's bright eyes dimmed as he looked around, seeking affirmation from others but finding none. That moment wasn't just about a disputed memory; it marked the beginning of Lucas's deep-seated doubt in his own perceptions.

As he grew older, these incidents became more frequent. His mother's words, laced with feigned concern and subtle accusations, made him question his memories, his decisions and even his feelings. "Are you sure you feel that way, Lucas? You are too sensitive," she would often say, dismissing his emotions as if they were figments of his imagination.

Each such interaction left Lucas feeling more isolated, his confidence slowly eroding. He started to believe that perhaps he was too sensitive, too forgetful, too emotional. His mother, always playing the role of the concerned caretaker, continued to erode his trust in himself, while positioning herself as his only reliable guide in a world she painted as confusing and hostile.

It wasn't until his first year of college, away from the stifling environment of his childhood home, that Lucas saw the manipulation for what it was. A conversation with a psychology professor opened his eyes to the term 'gaslighting,' a revelation that began his journey towards healing and understanding.

As we move through this chapter, our goal is twofold: To dissect the mechanics of gaslighting and to illuminate its subtle yet profound impact on the psyche. We will navigate through its various manifestations, understanding how it warps reality and erodes the autonomy of its targets. This journey is not merely academic; it is an essential step towards empowerment and healing.

This exploration is an invitation to you to join me in shedding light on this dark facet of human interaction. We will draw from stories like Lucas's, which exemplify the resilience and strength required to overcome the turmoil of gaslighting. Together, we embark on this path not just for understanding, but for regaining trust in ourselves and our perception of the world.

As we move through this chapter, remember that the journey of understanding gaslighting is also a journey towards reclaiming your reality and autonomy. It's about recognizing when your truth is being distorted and learning to anchor yourself firmly in your own experiences and perceptions. Let us begin this journey of enlightenment, understanding, and ultimately, self-empowerment.

The Mechanics of Gaslighting

Gaslighting is like a slow poison, a psychological manipulation that gradually erodes an individual's trust in their own perception and memory. Employed often with malicious intent, gaslighters seek to destabilize and control their target by distorting reality. In the story of Lucas, haunted by his mother's manipulations, we see a vivid example of this. Each time he confronts her about past incidents, she denies them or insists he's misremembering, planting seeds of doubt that make him question his memory and judgment.

Not just about denying facts, gaslighting also involves trivialization of the victim's feelings. When Lucas expresses how certain behaviors make him feel, he is met with dismissive comments like "You're too sensitive," or "You're overreacting." This tactic invalidates his emotions, leaving him wrestling with his sense of reality, further blurring the lines between what's true and what's been manipulated.

Blame-shifting is another tool in the gaslighter's arsenal, clear in Lucas's interactions with his mother. Every time he tries to talk about problems, he ends up being unfairly blamed. This ability to turn the tables and make Lucas feel guilty is a classic example of gaslighting, manipulating the victim into questioning their own actions and thoughts.

Projection is a subtle yet effective technique used in gaslighting. Lucas often finds himself accused of behaviors and attitudes that he doesn't exhibit but which are actually characteristics of his mother. This projection not only confuses him but also shifts the focus away from his mother's actions, making it harder for him to pinpoint the source of his discomfort.

In gaslighting, information is power. By withholding information and creating false narratives, the gaslighter constructs an alternative reality that further destabilizes the victim's sense of truth. Lucas experiences this through the selective omission of crucial details and the fabrication of stories by his mother, deepening his dependency on her to understand his own reality.

The emotional rollercoasters in gaslighting, where warmth and hostility are displayed interchangeably, keep the victim in a perpetual state of emotional confusion. Lucas experiences moments of affection from his mother, followed by cold indifference. This pattern leaves him uncertain about her feelings and his own, trapping him in a cycle of trying to decipher the unpredictable emotional landscape of their relationship.

Over time, constant criticism and ridicule eroded Lucas's self-esteem and confidence, especially regarding his thoughts and capabilities. Undermining his confidence is a slow and steady process, characteristic of gaslighting. As his self-assurance dwindles, he becomes more isolated, his mother cutting him off from external support systems. This isolation increases his reliance on her, further entrenching him in the manipulated reality she creates.

It's not an overnight transformation but a slow erosion of the victim's trust in their own senses. The long-term effects of prolonged exposure to gaslighting are severe. Loss of self-trust, anxiety, depression, isolation, and even physical symptoms are common. For Lucas, this manifested as trust issues, problems with self-esteem, and a distorted sense of self.

Recognizing it is the first step towards breaking free from its effects, enabling victims to seek the support they need to reclaim their sense of reality and autonomy.

Consequences of Gaslighting: Unraveling the Deep Emotional Scars

A central impact of gaslighting, vividly illustrated in Lucas's experience, is the profound erosion of self-trust. Constantly bombarded with messages that his perceptions were incorrect, Lucas, like many victims, began to doubt his sanity. This loss of confidence in one's own judgment and memories creates a dangerous dependency on the gaslighter, giving them immense control over the victim's reality. This diminished sense of autonomy is a key aspect of gaslighting's impact, as noted in research like that of Thakur (2021). It's not merely about losing trust in ourselves, but also about becoming unwittingly reliant on the very source of one's distress.

The effects of prolonged gaslighting extend far beyond the immediate psychological turmoil; they seep into every facet of the victim's life, manifesting in various distressing forms.

Psychological Turmoil: Anxiety, Depression, and Beyond

Gaslighting victims often find themselves enveloped in a fog of anxiety and stress. Lucas's constant second-guessing and fear of misinterpretation became a source of chronic stress, leading to heightened anxiety. The stress of dealing with gaslighting can lead to chronic anxiety, where the victim is perpetually on edge, bracing for the next wave of manipulation and confusion. This anxiety, coupled with the emotional abuse and self-doubt, often leads to depression. Victims may experience deep feelings of worthlessness and sadness as they grapple with their eroded self-esteem.

The isolation inflicted further compounds these effects. Lucas's gradual withdrawal from external relationships exacerbated the gaslighting effects. This social isolation deprives victims of essential external support and validation. Additionally, the prolonged stress and anxiety manifest in physical symptoms, like headaches, gastrointestinal issues, insomnia, and other stress-related health problems. These physical symptoms underscore the inextricable link between psychological distress and physical health.

The story of Lucas also highlights the long-term psychological trauma resulting from gaslighting. Symptoms akin to PTSD, such as flashbacks and heightened anxiety, are common among victims who have endured prolonged manipulation. This trauma extends to future relationships, where trust issues and emotional scars can create significant barriers to forming new, healthy connections. Victims often struggle to engage in open and trusting relationships due to their fear of past abuse recurring.

Recognizing and Overcoming Gaslighting

It is essential to pause and reflect on the complex tapestry of psychological manipulation we have explored. Our deep dive into the world of subtle emotional control, exemplified through the poignant narrative of Lucas, has revealed the multifaceted nature of this form of abuse. It has shown us how such tactics can significantly impact individuals, leaving them with deep emotional wounds and a fractured perception of their reality.

This form of manipulation is not merely a collection of random incidents, but a calculated approach to systematically dismantle an individual's confidence and self-belief. Employing a variety of tactics like denial, contradiction, and fluctuating emotional responses, manipulators skillfully erode their victim's trust in their own judgment. This results in a profound loss of personal confidence, accompanied by heightened feelings of anxiety, episodes of depression, and an overwhelming sense of being disconnected from one's surroundings. The physical and mental consequences of enduring such a sustained psychological assault can manifest in many ways, ranging from persistent stress to enduring emotional scars.

As we transition into the next chapter, we carry forward the valuable lessons and understanding gleaned from our exploration of psychological manipulation. Comprehending these manipulation tactics is fundamental to understanding the broader dynamics at play in toxic relationships. The upcoming chapter promises to delve deeper into the emotional aftermath of such relationships, providing perspectives on coping strategies and pathways to emotional healing. Our exploration has equipped us with essential knowledge to understand and address the intricate emotional landscapes carved out by toxic dynamics.

It becomes clear that the type of emotional abuse discussed here is a powerful and damaging phenomenon. Its influence on an individual's mental health and interpersonal relationships is profound, making the journey to recovery both challenging and essential. By acknowledging and addressing these manipulative behaviors, individuals empower themselves to reclaim control over their reality, embarking on a path toward emotional healing, resilience, and a renewed sense of empowerment.

Chapter 5:

The Emotional Impact of Toxic Relationships

Bad relationships change good people. —Shubbu

Once buoyant and self-assured, Alex found himself engulfed in the suffocating embrace of a toxic marriage. His partner's unrelenting criticism and manipulative tactics slowly chipped away at his self-esteem, leaving him feeling powerless and ensnared. This relationship's emotional toll manifested in profound ways—from the dimming of his once-vibrant spirit to the onset of anxiety and depression. This decline was further accelerated by his increasing isolation from friends and family, a withdrawal stemming from a misplaced belief that he deserved such derogatory treatment.

Alex's story is more than a personal narrative; it is a reflection of the experiences shared by many in similar predicaments. It shows how toxic relationships can warp our sense of reality, leading to diminished self-worth and escalating emotional turmoil. His journey, marked by the complexities of such a relationship, underscores the critical need for understanding and addressing these impacts for emotional recovery and healing.

As we navigate this chapter, we will dissect various aspects of the emotional impact of toxic relationships. We will delve into the constant companions of anxiety and stress and the insidious creep of depression and diminished self-esteem. We will traverse the emotional rollercoaster that these relationships often entail; namely, the fleeting highs of sporadic affection and the profound lows of persistent devaluation.

Through Alex's story and the experiences of countless others, this chapter seeks to provide a comprehensive overview of the emotional landscape sculpted by toxic relationships. Our goal is to equip readers with the insights needed to recognize, comprehend, and ultimately, embark on the path to recovery and healing from the emotional scars these relationships leave behind.

The Cycle of Emotional Turmoil

This cycle represents a pervasive pattern of emotional responses that are both a symptom and a consequence of being in a toxic relationship. Through the lens of Alex's experiences, we will explore how this cycle manifests and the profound impact it has on the mental and emotional state.

Anxiety and Constant Stress: The Persistent Shadow

Anxiety and stress are not fleeting emotions but persistent shadows that significantly affect both emotional and physical health. Individuals like Alex, caught in the tumult of such relationships, find themselves in a state of perpetual unease and apprehension. The chronic nature of this stress, stemming from the unpredictability and volatility of toxic dynamics, places individuals in a state of constant vigilance. This relentless stress manifests in physical symptoms like insomnia, headaches, and gastrointestinal issues, disrupting the body's natural hormonal balance and potentially leading to long-term health problems.

The mental health implications of this continuous stress are profound. Living under constant anxiety can lead to anxiety disorders, exacerbate existing mental health issues, and impair one's ability to function effectively in daily life. The sensation of being entrapped in an abusive cycle, with its inherent unpredictability, amplifies the emotional turmoil, often leaving individuals feeling overwhelmed and powerless.

Depression and Low Self-Esteem: The Insidious Consequences

The link between toxic relationships and the development of depression and low self-esteem is both direct and insidious. The constant barrage of criticism, belittlement, and emotional manipulation chips away at an individual's sense of self-worth and identity. Over time, this erosion of self-esteem can spiral into deep feelings of hopelessness and despair.

Victims of toxic relationships often internalize the negative messages and treatment they receive. This leads to a distorted self-image and plummeting self-esteem, manifesting as depression, characterized by persistent sadness, loss of interest in activities once enjoyed, and a deep sense of worthlessness.

This depressive state in a toxic relationship is further intensified by isolation and emotional exhaustion. Withdrawal from social support networks, whether due to manipulation by the other or self-imposed isolation, exacerbates the feelings of loneliness and despair, deepening the cycle of emotional turmoil.

Emotional Rollercoaster: Navigating the Highs and Lows

Toxic relationships are often marked by a disorienting emotional rollercoaster consisting of alternating periods of affection and calm with conflict and emotional distress. This erratic pattern is incredibly disorienting and leaves individuals like Alex confused about their feelings and the overall state of the relationship.

During moments of calm, the toxic partner may exhibit affection and charm, creating a sense of happiness and false security. These periods are intensely gratifying, reinforcing the attachment to the relationship. However, these highs are inevitably followed by lows dominated by criticism, hostility, and emotional abuse.

This fluctuation creates a confusing and exhausting emotional landscape, where victims are in a constant state of uncertainty and apprehension. This cycle of hope and despair complicates decision-making about the relationship and personal well-being, making it challenging for individuals to see a clear path forward.

Understanding this emotional rollercoaster is vital for individuals in toxic relationships. It provides insight into the complex emotions experienced and is a crucial step towards seeking help and breaking free from the cycle.

Isolation and Loneliness

The tools of isolation and emotional manipulation are wielded with precision, often leaving individuals cut off from their support networks and engulfed in profound loneliness. This isolation, both physical and emotional, exacerbates the emotional toll and deepens the sense of entrapment.

Toxic dynamics often involve a calculated effort to isolate the individual from their friends, family, and any external support system. This isolation is strategically designed to increase the victim's dependency on the toxic partner. For someone like Alex, this might manifest as his partner, criticizing his friends and family or creating situations that make social interactions challenging or unpleasant. Consequently, individuals find themselves increasingly alienated, their world contracting until it orbits solely around the toxic relationship.

This isolation is particularly damaging, as it not only deprives individuals of much-needed emotional support but also distorts their perception of the relationship. Cut off from external perspectives, they become more susceptible to the manipulative narratives spun by their toxic partners. This lack of external validation leaves them feeling trapped and powerless, exacerbating the emotional distress inherent in the relationship.

Emotional Loneliness: The Paradox of Isolation in Company

Emotional loneliness represents a unique challenge. It is the paradoxical state of feeling profoundly alone and disconnected, even in the physical company of the toxic partner. This form of loneliness stems from the absence of genuine emotional intimacy and understanding within the relationship. The constant conflict, criticism, and emotional abuse create a chasm between the individuals, leaving one feeling unseen, unheard, and emotionally abandoned.

This emotional loneliness is particularly insidious, as it can persist even amidst superficial togetherness. Victims may share a home, social engagements, and daily routines with the toxic partner yet experience an overwhelming sense of emotional isolation. This disconnection can have far-reaching implications, affecting mental health, self-esteem, and overall sense of well-being.

Codependency and Identity Loss: The Erosion of Self

Codependency often emerges as a coping mechanism, where the individual becomes excessively preoccupied with the needs and problems of the toxic partner, often at the expense of their own well-being and identity. This codependency results in a loss of personal identity, as the individual's thoughts, feelings, and actions become increasingly aligned with the desires and demands of their partner.

The impact of codependency on emotional health is profound. It leads to a sense of identity loss, where individuals no longer recognize themselves or their own needs and desires. They become an extension of their partner, with their goals and aspirations submerged by the relationship. This loss of self can lead to deep emotional turmoil, including feelings of emptiness, despair, and a pervasive sense of being lost.

Moreover, codependency perpetuates the cycle of toxicity. The individual's lack of autonomy and self-identity makes it challenging to break free from the relationship, reinforcing their feelings of helplessness and hopelessness. The emotional toll of codependency is a significant aspect that needs us to recognize in order to overcome.

Powerlessness and Helplessness

For someone like Alex, entangled in a toxic marriage, this manifests as a constant, debilitating sense of helplessness. It often results from enduring manipulation, emotional abuse, and systematic undermining of self-esteem. Individuals feel stuck, unable to see a life beyond the confines of their toxic relationship. This feeling of entrapment stems from a mix of fear, emotional dependency, and a belief in the lack of viable alternatives.

The sense of powerlessness is further exacerbated by the dynamics of the relationship itself. Tactics such as threats, emotional blackmail, or gaslighting are used by the toxic partner to maintain control and keep the individual in a submissive state. As a result, the victim feels unable to assert themselves, make independent decisions, or take steps towards exiting the relationship, deepening the feelings of helplessness.

Learned Helplessness: A Psychological Trap

The concept of learned helplessness, as described by psychologists Martin Seligman and Steven Maier, offers a lens to understand how individuals in toxic relationships might come to accept their situation as unchangeable. Learned helplessness occurs when an individual, after repeated exposure to aversive and uncontrollable events, learns to believe that they have no control over their circumstances. This belief leads to passive acceptance of the situation, even when opportunities for change are available.

In toxic relationships, learned helplessness manifests as resignation to ongoing abuse and manipulation. Individuals may believe that any effort to improve the situation or leave the relationship is futile, leading to a state of resignation and inactivity. This psychological state not only perpetuates the cycle of abuse but also hinders the individual's ability to seek help or envision a life beyond the toxic environment.

Coping Mechanisms and Self-Destructive Behavior

To manage the overwhelming stress and emotional pain of a toxic relationship, individuals may resort to self-destructive coping mechanisms. While these behaviors provide temporary relief or distraction, they can have detrimental long-term effects on mental and physical health.

Common self-destructive coping mechanisms include substance abuse, self-harm, and engaging in risky behaviors. Substance abuse, for example, can offer a temporary escape from the emotional turmoil but often leads to addiction and further emotional instability. Similarly, self-harm, such as cutting or burning, may act as a physical outlet for internal pain and a way to exert control in a situation where control is otherwise lacking.

These coping strategies reflect the profound distress experienced in toxic relationships. They are cries for help, signaling the desperation and hopelessness felt by the individual. Recognizing and addressing these self-destructive behaviors is a crucial step in the journey towards healing from a toxic relationship. Seeking professional help and establishing healthy coping strategies are vital in breaking free from the cycle of self-destruction and reclaiming control over one's life.

Emotional Trauma

Emotional trauma often results from a prolonged exposure to emotional abuse, manipulation, and neglect. It represents a psychological injury that disrupts an individual's sense of security, rendering them vulnerable, helpless, and often profoundly alone. Unlike trauma from a single event, this trauma is insidious, stemming from a cumulative erosion of the self.

Individuals like Alex may experience various manifestations of this trauma, including pervasive sadness or despair, intrusive thoughts about the relationship, and difficulty in trusting others. There might also be a persistent sense of fear or anxiety, particularly in contexts reminiscent of the toxic relationship.

Identifying Symptoms and Effects

The aftermath of enduring a toxic relationship often manifests as emotional trauma, a complex psychological condition's life. Recognizing the multifaceted symptoms and effects of this trauma is crucial for the journey towards healing and recovery.

- **Flashbacks and Intrusive Thoughts:** One of the most striking symptoms is the presence of flashbacks and intrusive thoughts. Individuals may relive painful memories or specific moments from the toxic relationship, often unexpectedly. These flashbacks can be vivid and emotionally intense, disrupting daily life and causing significant distress.

- **Hyperarousal:** Hyperarousal, or a constant state of heightened anxiety, is another common symptom. This may manifest as an exaggerated startle response, irritability, or a pervasive feeling of being on edge. Individuals may struggle with sleep disturbances, have a quick temper, or find themselves constantly vigilant, as if waiting for something negative to happen.

- **Avoidance:** Avoidance behaviors are a key indicator of emotional trauma. Individuals may actively avoid places, people, or activities that remind them of the toxic relationship. This avoidance can lead to social withdrawal, isolation, and a narrowing of one's life experiences, as they steer clear of situations that trigger painful memories.

- **Negative Changes in Thoughts and Mood:** Emotional trauma often brings about profound changes in thoughts and mood. Persistent negative beliefs about oneself or the world, feelings of hopelessness, and a loss of interest in activities once enjoyed are common. This shift in mood and thinking can affect every aspect of life, leading to a general sense of despair and disconnection.

- **Emotional Numbness:** Emotional numbness, or detachment from emotions, is a coping mechanism that some individuals develop. It involves a sense of feeling emotionally 'flat,' disconnected from others, or unable to access one's own emotions. This numbness can be protective in the short term but can hinder emotional processing and recovery in the long run.

- **Physical Symptoms:** Emotional trauma can have physical manifestations as well. Stress-related ailments such as headaches, gastrointestinal issues, chronic fatigue, or muscle tension are often observed. These physical symptoms, which often have no apparent medical cause, can be debilitating and further complicate the healing process.

- **Difficulty in Forming New Relationships:** Emotional trauma can significantly impact an individual's ability to form new, healthy relationships. Trust issues, fear of intimacy, or an overarching fear of being hurt again can make it challenging to connect with others. This can lead to a cycle of loneliness and isolation, as the individual may find it hard to engage in new relationships.

Recognizing these symptoms and understanding their effects is a vital step in acknowledging the depth and reality of emotional trauma. This awareness is the foundation upon which healing and recovery can be built. It opens the door to seeking appropriate support, whether through therapy, support groups, or other healing modalities, and marks the beginning of the journey towards reclaiming one's life and emotional well-being.

Healing and Moving Forward

Healing from emotional trauma is a gradual and often challenging process. It entails acknowledging the pain, understanding its roots, and actively working towards emotional recovery. Key steps include seeking professional therapy, building a supportive network of friends and family, and developing healthy coping strategies. The aim is to process the trauma, rebuild a sense of safety and trust, and empower the individual to reclaim control over their life and well-being.

From the persistent cycle of emotional turmoil to the depths of isolation and loneliness, the effects are complex and devastating. The feelings of powerlessness and helplessness, often culminating in learned helplessness and self-destructive coping mechanisms, underscore the depth of despair experienced in such relationships. The culmination of these experiences often results in emotional trauma, a lasting scar affecting every facet of one's life.

This chapter has been a journey of uncovering the harsh realities faced by individuals like Alex in toxic relationships. It has underscored the importance of recognizing these dynamics as a crucial first step towards healing and recovery. Understanding the emotional impact is essential in validating the experiences of those who have suffered and providing a roadmap for their journey towards healing.

As we transition to the next chapter, we carry forward the insights gained. This knowledge is instrumental in framing our approach to recovery and resilience. We will dive into the transformative process of healing, exploring strategies to overcome the past and build a future grounded in self-awareness, strength, and emotional well-being. Our exploration continues, focusing now on turning adversity into a steppingstone for personal growth and empowerment.

Section 2:

Strategies

Chapter 6:

Choosing Your Path: Stay or Go?

Should I stay or should I go now? If I stay, it will be trouble; if I go, it will be double...—The Clash

These iconic lyrics resonate deeply with the heart of this chapter. When ensnared in the web of a toxic relationship, the decision to stay becomes a complex maze of emotions, fears, and often misguided hopes. To fully grasp this dilemma, we must delve into the intricate dynamics of such relationships, the internal conflicts they engender, and the elusive signs of hope that often keep individuals anchored in turbulent waters.

The Harrowing Dynamics of Toxic Relationships

Individuals trapped in toxic relationships often find themselves ensnared by a triad of harmful behaviors: emotional manipulation, control, and gaslighting. Each contributes to a distressing environment where one's sense of self and reality is persistently compromised.

Emotional manipulation emerges as a key tactic, with emotions strategically used to shape and influence the partner's behavior. Tactics like guilt-tripping or love-bombing create an environment of emotional dependence, blurring the lines between affection and manipulation. This often leaves victims in a state of continual confusion, torn between their emotional attachment and the pain caused by manipulative behaviors.

Control is another cornerstone of these relationships, manifesting in both overt and covert forms. Controlling partners may overtly dictate decisions or subtly impose psychological constraints, effectively isolating victims from their support systems and dominating the relationship's narrative. Such control tactics significantly undermine the victim's autonomy, often leaving them feeling helpless and overly reliant on their partner.

Employing tactics such as denial, contradiction, and misinformation, gaslighters cause victims to doubt their memories and judgment. This psychological manipulation is especially harmful, as it can lead victims to question their sanity and the validity of their perceptions, resulting in profound disorientation and uncertainty.

Navigating the Internal Conflicts

Staying often leads us into a whirlpool of internal conflicts. Attachment to the abuser, despite the toxicity, is a common struggle. Emotional bonds, sometimes formed over years, create a powerful tether, making it difficult to envision life separate from the relationship. This attachment is often rooted in a mix of love, habit, and fear.

Fear plays a significant role in the staying dilemma. Fear of the unknown, fear of being alone, or fear of retaliation from the partner can be paralyzing. Additionally, the history of the relationship, marked by cycles of abuse and reconciliation, fosters uncertainty and fear of making the wrong decision.

Compounding these fears is the pervasive self-doubt instilled by the toxic dynamics of the relationship. Victims often struggle with feelings of inadequacy and low self-worth, questioning their ability to survive outside the relationship.

In such turmoil, victims often cling to signs of hope, however fleeting. Occasional remorse from the toxic partner can be seen as a signal of potential change. Initiatives like counseling or therapy by the partner may appear as steps toward improvement. Sometimes, it's the victim's own resilience that fuels hope, nurturing a belief that they can endure and catalyze change within the relationship.

However, these signs of hope can be double-edged swords. They offer respite from relentless negativity and serve as a justification for staying. Yet, they can also prolong exposure to the harmful environment, delaying the decision to seek a healthier path.

Understanding the staying dilemma in toxic relationships involves unraveling the complex interplay of harmful dynamics, internal conflicts, and the fragile threads of hope that bind victims to their abusers. It's a journey requiring not only deepen understanding but also compassionate acknowledgment of the emotional turmoil involved in the choice to stay or leave. As we proceed through this chapter, we aim to provide insights and guidance to those facing this dilemma, offering a path toward clarity and empowerment.

Exploring the Option to Leave

Deciding to leave a toxic relationship is a pivotal moment in anyone's life. It's a profound act of transformation and self-assertion, demanding not just an evaluation of the relationship's impact on one's safety and well-being but also a careful, strategic plan for the future. This decision, often made in the depths of emotional turmoil, marks the beginning of a journey towards reclaiming one's autonomy and sense of self.

The path to this decision is complex. For many, like Alex, it starts with the stark realization that the toxic environment has significantly compromised their personal safety and emotional health. Consider the case where emotional or physical abuse escalates, where every day is marked by a persistent cloud of fear and anxiety. Such an environment can lead to a general sense of erosion in mental and emotional well-being. Imagine waking up every day to a world where your sense of self is constantly under attack, where the very foundation of your identity is shaken by continual belittlement and manipulation. This is the harsh reality for those trapped in toxic relationships, where staying often becomes untenable as the relationship persistently undermines their sense of self and security.

The critical step in leaving is gathering resources, which encompasses more than just physical preparation. It's about building a safety net that can support the transition away from toxicity. For someone like Alex, this might mean reaching out to trusted friends or family for a safe place to stay, or it could involve seeking safe housing options independently. Financial independence is a crucial aspect of this stage. Imagine the challenge of setting up separate bank accounts and developing a sustainable budget, perhaps for the first time in years. For some, this might even involve seeking financial advice or assistance. Alongside financial and physical safety planning, building a supportive network is indispensable. This network, whether it's friends, family, or support groups, provides emotional sustenance and practical help during one of life's most challenging transitions.

Professional help often plays a critical role in navigating the complexities of leaving a toxic relationship. Therapy or counseling can offer a safe and supportive space to confront the fears and anxieties that accompany such a significant change. Through professional guidance, individuals can gain clarity on the factors involved in their decision and develop a structured plan for departure. Therapists can help untangle the web of emotions tied to the relationship and strategize a departure that prioritizes personal safety and emotional well-being. They can support individuals in preparing not just logistically but also emotionally for the road ahead.

Leaving a toxic relationship is never just about the physical act of departure; it's about embarking on a path toward self-recovery. It's about stepping into a future where safety, independence, and emotional health are paramount. This journey, while daunting, is a testament to the resilience of the human spirit. It's a step towards breaking free from the chains of toxicity and moving towards a life characterized by autonomy, strength, and well-being.

We will delve into the emotional, psychological, and practical considerations that come into play, offering insights and guidance to those standing at these crossroads. It's a journey that intertwines self-awareness, careful planning, and emotional resilience, leading towards a new chapter of life filled with hope and empowerment.

The Middle Ground: Temporary Separation

In this challenging path, individuals often find themselves at a crucial turning point where finding a compromise becomes crucial. Viewing this middle ground as a temporary separation can be a vital step. It offers a pause from the overwhelming immediacy of the relationship's challenges, providing a space for clarity, introspection, and, importantly, healing.

Temporary separation is more than just physical distance; it's a conscious decision to step back and reassess the dynamics of the relationship from a clearer, more detached perspective. For someone like James, who constantly oscillated between hope and despair in his tumultuous marriage, choosing a temporary separation was a momentous decision. It allowed him to step out of the daily emotional chaos and evaluate his feelings, needs, and the overall health of his relationship without the direct influence of his partner's manipulative behaviors. This break became a period of significant clarity and self-reflection, enabling James to see the patterns and cycles that had kept him anchored in the relationship for so long.

The process of temporary separation is as much about setting boundaries as it is about physical distance. Establishing and adhering to these boundaries is crucial for the separation to serve its purpose effectively. For James, this meant defining clear guidelines for communication with his partner, setting boundaries around personal space and interaction, and taking control of his individual daily routine. These boundaries were vital for maintaining his sense of autonomy and ensuring that the toxic dynamics of his relationship did not permeate this period of separation. He communicated these boundaries to his partner, ensuring that both parties were clear about the terms of their time apart.

During this time of separation, individuals often experience a unique opportunity for personal growth and emotional healing. Away from the constant stressors and conflicts of their toxic relationship, they can focus on their well-being and personal development. This period can be a time for engaging in self-care practices, reconnecting with personal interests, or even rediscovering aspects of oneself that may have been overshadowed by the relationship. For James, the separation was a time of significant introspection. He understood his values, needs, and desires more clearly, and reassessed the role his relationship played in fulfilling—or hindering—these aspects of his life. It was also a period for him to process the accumulated hurt and confusion, often with the support of therapy or counseling. He rebuilt his sense of identity, independent of his partner's influence, emerging more self-aware and emotionally resilient.

Yet, temporary separation isn't just a journey of individual self-discovery; it's also a litmus test for the relationship itself. It reveals the true nature of the dynamics between partners. In James's case, the separation laid bare the extent of manipulation and control that had characterized his marriage. It provided him with the perspective needed to evaluate whether positive change was possible, or if a more permanent departure was the healthier choice.

Navigating a temporary separation is about striking a balance between introspective self-evaluation and practical reassessment of the relationship. It's about taking a step back to gain a clearer, more objective view of one's situation and what one truly desires from a relationship. For many, like James, this period can be transformative, leading to profound personal growth and a deeper understanding of their needs and aspirations. It is a critical step in the decision-making process, offering insights that can guide whether to stay, leave, or seek a different path altogether.

As we transition to the next phase of our exploration, the journey continues with a focus on understanding and navigating these critical crossroads in toxic relationships. It's about harnessing the insights gained during separation to make empowered decisions that lead towards a future defined by emotional well-being, independence, and healthier relational dynamics.

Making the Decision

When confronted with the crucial decision of whether to stay in or leave a toxic relationship, the process is far from straightforward. It's a path marked by deep introspection, careful evaluation, and often, the courage to trust one's deeper instincts. This decision-making journey transcends gender, sexual orientation, and cultural backgrounds, as it's a universal challenge faced by anyone in a toxic dynamic.

Consider the story of Jordan, caught in a toxic relationship with a partner who oscillated between emotional manipulation and moments of affection. For Jordan, the decision to stay or leave involved an intricate balance of rational assessment and emotional introspection. He embarked on a journey of meticulously weighing the pros and cons, examining not just the immediate effects of his relationship but also its long-term implications in his life. He thought about their shared experiences and the potential for change, yet also faced the stark reality of ongoing emotional abuse and its toll on his mental health.

Simultaneously, Jordan grappled with his intuition. He listened attentively to his inner voice, which often revealed truths that the rational mind overlooked. This intuition served as a guide, highlighting the emotional impact of the relationship on his well-being. He learned to trust these feelings, understanding that they were crucial in guiding him towards a decision that resonated with his core values and needs.

Seeking professional guidance played a pivotal role in Jordan's journey. Sessions with a therapist provided a safe space to untangle the complex emotions and fears surrounding his decision. The therapist offered insights into the patterns of behavior in the relationship, like the cycles of control and dependency, and helped Jordan develop strategies to cope with the change, whether he stayed and work on the relationship or to leave and embark on a new path.

In diverse toxic dynamics, the decision to stay or leave is not confined to romantic relationships alone. It could involve family relationships, friendships, or professional connections. The principles of careful evaluation, listening to one's instincts, and seeking professional help remain consistent across these various contexts.

Let's always remember that deciding to stay or leave a toxic relationship is a multifaceted and deeply personal process. It involves a balanced evaluation of the relationship's impact, an attentive listening to one's inner voice, and often the guidance of a mental health professional. This comprehensive approach ensures that the decision is not just rational but also emotionally intelligent, leading to a choice that aligns with the individual's unique circumstances, needs, and aspirations for the future. Whether it's Jordan or anyone else navigating this path, the journey, while complex, is a powerful stride towards personal growth, emotional freedom, and a healthier future.

Moving Forward, Regardless of the Choice

Reaching the decision to stay or leave marks not just an end, but the beginning of a new chapter. This crucial turning point, regardless of the path chosen, heralds a period of transformation that needs a deep dive into emotional readiness, the cultivation of a strong support network, and a dedicated commitment to the process of recovery and healing.

Embarking on this path after making such a significant decision, individuals navigate a complex emotional terrain. This period is often marked by a mix of relief, uncertainty, and introspection. For those like Daniel, who stayed and worked on his relationship, it meant bracing for the emotional work ahead, cultivating resilience to face the challenges of improving the dynamics with his partner. Conversely, for Emma, who left, it involved preparing for the emotional upheaval of stepping into a new, independent life. Both paths require fortifying one's emotional strength, developing coping strategies to manage the stress, anxiety, and grief that might accompany their decision. Practices like mindfulness, journaling, and engaging in reflective activities become key tools in navigating this emotional journey.

An essential element in moving forward is the support system that one builds. A nurturing and understanding network is essential, regardless of whether one stays or leaves. They offer a pillar of strength, providing emotional support, practical advice, and a sense of belonging during a period that can often feel overwhelming and isolating. In Daniel's case, his friends and a therapist provided him with perspectives that helped him stay grounded and focused on his well-being as he worked through the relationship. For Emma, her support network was instrumental in offering safety, resources, and a buffer against the potential repercussions of her departure.

Irrespective of the decision to stay or leave, the journey towards recovery and healing is a personal path of growth. It involves rediscovering and reaffirming one's self-identity, self-esteem, and autonomy. If the decision is to stay, as in Daniel's case, the focus might be on rebuilding trust, establishing healthier communication patterns, and nurturing individual and joint growth within the relationship. For those who, like Emma, choose to leave, the journey might center on rediscovering personal interests, re-establishing independence, and redefining life's path. It's a transformative period where individuals learn from their experiences, foster self-awareness, and gradually work towards a future that resonates with their deepest values and aspirations.

Ultimately, moving forward after deciding to stay in or leave a toxic relationship is a deeply personal and often challenging journey. It demands emotional resilience, a supportive environment, and a steadfast commitment to recovery and healing. Whether the decision is to stay and seek improvement or to leave and start afresh, this journey is about growth, healing, and rediscovering a life that echoes with one's true self. It's a path that, though fraught with challenges, offers the promise of a more fulfilling and authentic existence, a testament to the enduring strength and resilience of the human spirit.

Chapter 7:

Healing and Recovery: Reclaiming Your Emotional Well-Being

As you remove toxic people from your life, you free up space and emotional energy for positive, healthy relationships.
—John Mark Green

Here we find a profound truth that resonates with anyone who has embarked on the challenging path away from a toxic relationship. This chapter is dedicated to guiding you through the process of healing and recovery, aiming to help you reclaim your emotional well-being and foster a brighter, healthier future.

Consider the story of Jamal, whose journey symbolizes a new beginning rather than an end. His decision to leave a toxic relationship marked the start of a profound journey into self-discovery and healing. For Jamal, this path was not just about leaving a detrimental situation; it was about embarking on a transformative journey towards rediscovering himself. He faced many challenges along the way, but each step he took was a stride towards a renewed sense of self. With therapy and self-reflection as his guiding lights, Jamal rekindled the joys of friendships and hobbies that had been overshadowed by the turmoil of his past relationship. His healing journey was gradual, acknowledging that the scars of emotional abuse don't fade overnight. Yet, he found strength in the quieter moments of his journey, embracing the tranquility that replaced the former chaos. Jamal's heart, once heavy with the burden of a toxic past, slowly learned to beat to the rhythm of self-love and hope.

Jamal's story reflects the experiences of many who bravely walk away from toxic relationships. It's a testament to the resilience of the human spirit and its remarkable capacity for healing and renewal. In this chapter, we will explore strategies and insights to navigate the intricate emotions and challenges that accompany the healing process. You will find guidance on nurturing self-compassion, rebuilding self-esteem, and forging a path to a life filled with positive, fulfilling relationships. This journey of healing is a reaffirmation of one's strength and an opportunity to reshape one's future into something brighter and more hopeful.

Through this exploration, the aim is to provide you with the tools and understanding necessary for a holistic recovery. The journey might be complex and layered, but it holds the promise of leading to a more fulfilling, authentic existence, one where emotional well-being and personal growth are at the forefront. The path to healing is not just about moving past a toxic relationship; it's about stepping into a space of empowerment and rediscovery, where each step forward is a step towards a life of greater joy, peace, and fulfillment.

Acknowledging and Validating Your Pain

Healing begins with a critical first step: acknowledging and validating the emotional toll it has taken. This involves confronting and accepting the feelings of pain, anger, and grief that inevitably surface. The emotional scars left by toxic relationships, characterized by manipulation, betrayal, and emotional abuse, are profound and understanding them is essential for healing.

Toxic relationships can profoundly impact mental health and emotional well-being, sometimes leading to PTSD, flashbacks, anxiety, depression, or unexpected triggers that recall painful memories. Take Jamal's experience, for example. His path, like that of many others, was fraught with these emotional battles, illustrating the deep-seated effects of prolonged exposure to a toxic dynamic.

These emotional responses are natural reactions to the unnatural environment of a toxic relationship. The emotional rollercoaster—the highs of temporary affection followed by the lows of mistreatment—often leaves a lasting state of emotional flux, persisting even after the relationship has ended.

Validating your feelings and experiences is a significant step in the healing process. In toxic relationships, where gaslighting and manipulation are common, your emotions and perceptions may have been consistently invalidated, leading to self-doubt. Reclaiming your truth starts with acknowledging that your emotions are valid and real. Techniques like journaling or mindfulness meditation can help to process and understand your emotions. Positive self-talk, replacing self-criticism with affirmations and compassionate language, is also crucial.

Seeking therapy or counseling is another important aspect of this validation process. Professional guidance offers a safe space to explore and affirm your experiences and emotions. Therapists are skilled in helping individuals navigate the complex web of feelings resulting from toxic relationships and offer strategies for managing and overcoming them.

Confiding in trusted friends, family, or therapists about your experiences can be tremendously beneficial. Sharing your reality with others not only helps validate your experiences, but also provides emotional support. An external perspective, especially from those who care about you or from professionals who understand toxic relationship dynamics, can be both affirming and healing, as Jamal found in his journey. The support and understanding he received from his therapist and close friends were vital, providing him with the strength to continue on his path toward healing.

Acknowledging and validating your pain is the foundational step toward healing from a toxic relationship. It's about recognizing the impact of the relationship on your emotional well-being, affirming the reality of your experiences, and seeking the support to embark on the path to recovery. This step, while challenging, is essential to pave the way towards reclaiming your emotional health and well-being.

Strategies for Emotional Recovery

Emotional recovery is like an expedition, where we find both obstacles and life-changing epiphanies. Central to this healing process are therapy, the cultivation of self-esteem, and learning to cope with emotional triggers, each playing a vital role in the transition to well-being.

In the realm of therapy, the significance of a safe and nonjudgmental space becomes immediately apparent. Here, individuals like Jamal find the freedom to unravel their complex web of emotions, which may range from deep-seated betrayal to pervasive grief. Therapy, especially with a professional specializing in trauma recovery, offers a unique environment where one can dissect these feelings and learn coping strategies. Employing techniques from cognitive-behavioral therapy, dialectical behavior therapy, or mindfulness practices, therapy aids in navigating through the emotional aftermath of toxic relationships.

Simultaneously, the journey of healing demands a reconstruction of eroded self-esteem and confidence. This reconstruction is not a mere reversal of past damages, but a proactive cultivation of self-worth and autonomy. It involves setting personal boundaries, a crucial practice that helps re-establish one's sense of self and offers protection against potential emotional harm. Alongside boundary setting, nurturing self-compassion and self-love are essential. Practices such as positive self-affirmations, self-care routines, and celebrating personal achievements, however small, foster a renewed sense of self-worth and bolster confidence.

Another critical aspect of this journey is learning to manage emotional triggers. These triggers, remnants of the toxic relationship, can evoke intense emotional responses, often unexpectedly. Developing effective strategies to handle these triggers is crucial for sustained emotional recovery. Recognizing what sets off these triggers, engaging in stress-relief practices, and relying on supportive networks can make a significant difference. Emotional resilience becomes key here, empowering individuals to experience and process their emotions without being overwhelmed. This resilience is cultivated through mindfulness, self-reflection, and nurturing supportive relationships.

This multifaceted approach to emotional recovery, interweaving therapy, self-esteem rebuilding, and trigger management offers a comprehensive path for healing from the effects of toxic relationships. It's a journey that not only addresses the deep emotional impacts but also equips individuals with tools to navigate daily life post-relationship. Each step helps reclaim emotional health and steers life towards a future marked by stability, respect, and resilience.

Forgiveness and Letting Go

Healing from a toxic relationship often hinges on the powerful acts of forgiveness and letting go. This crucial phase of recovery is not about excusing the wrongs done by others, but about liberating from the lingering emotional pain that those experiences have caused.

The Essence of Forgiveness

Forgiveness is an act of self-liberation. It's about releasing the burden of resentment, anger, and bitterness that can consume your thoughts and hinder your emotional progress. This form of forgiveness doesn't imply overlooking the harmful actions or forgetting the pain inflicted. Instead, it's a conscious choice to prioritize your peace and emotional well-being over the hold of past grievances.

People often misinterpret the true meaning of forgiveness, as it does not equal reconciliation. It's more about a personal commitment to move past the pain, focusing on creating a positive and healthy future. The act of forgiving can be a steppingstone to emotional closure, facilitating a sense of inner peace and resolution.

Letting Go: The Path to Emotional Liberation

Letting go complements the process of forgiveness. It's an active decision to stop allowing past hurts to impact your present life. It's akin to unburdening yourself from the weight of negative emotions tied to past experiences. Letting go can involve a range of practices like mindfulness, which helps in staying anchored in the present, journaling to process and release emotions, or indulging in activities that foster joy and contentment. In therapy, you can find additional strategies and support to help in shedding these emotional burdens effectively.

Journeying Through Forgiveness

The journey through forgiveness is highly individual and often non-linear. It may encompass periods of anger and grief before reaching a state of tranquility. An essential part of this process is also learning to forgive oneself. It involves understanding that in the toxic relationship, your reactions and decisions were based on the situation at hand, and self-blame is not a burden you need to carry forward.

Patience is key in this journey. Whether through personal reflection, therapeutic interventions, or mindfulness practices, each step towards forgiveness is a stride toward emotional health and a future free from the shadows of past relationships. It's a gradual shift from dwelling on past hurts to embracing a life of emotional balance and well-being.

This approach to healing—embracing forgiveness and letting go—is not just about recovering from the past, but about building a foundation for a happier, more fulfilling future. It's a vital step in transforming the pain of a toxic relationship into a catalyst for personal growth and renewed emotional strength.

Rebuilding Trust and Healthy Relationships

In the aftermath of a toxic relationship, rebuilding self-trust becomes a crucial part of the recovery process. This phase is crucial because such relationships often leave you doubting your judgment and instincts. Rediscovering trust in your own decisions is about reconnecting with your intuition and affirming your capability to make sound choices. It's nurturing your self-confidence and relearning to rely on your inner voice for guidance.

This journey of self-trust involves various practices. Engaging in self-reflection is a powerful tool. It allows you to look inward, understand your thought processes, and recognize patterns that may have been shaped by the toxic relationship. It's about questioning old beliefs and reassessing your values and priorities.

Therapeutic support is often a key component in rebuilding this trust. A therapist can help you navigate your doubts and fears, offering insights and strategies to strengthen your trust in yourself. They provide an external, objective perspective that can be invaluable in challenging the negative self-perceptions formed in the toxic relationship.

Self-care practices play a significant role. Activities that reinforce your sense of self-worth, such as pursuing hobbies, setting personal goals, and celebrating your achievements, however small, contribute to rebuilding your confidence. These activities are not just pastimes, they are vital steps in affirming your abilities and worth.

As you gradually trust yourself more, you'll notice a shift in how you approach decisions and set boundaries in relationships. Decision-making becomes less daunting, and establishing boundaries feels more intuitive. This growing self-trust lays the foundation for healthier future relationships and a stronger sense of self.

Rebuilding trust in yourself after a toxic relationship is about rediscovering your strength and capabilities. It's a journey that requires patience, reflection, and often external support, but it leads to a more empowered and confident self, ready to face future challenges and embrace new opportunities with a renewed sense of trust and self-assurance.

Recognizing Healthy Relationships

When stepping out from the shadows, it becomes crucial to comprehend the elements that make up a healthy relationship. This understanding is a crucial step towards ensuring future relationships are founded on mutual respect, effective communication, and emotional safety. Healthy relationships are characterized by support for each other's growth and well-being, where conflicts are resolved constructively, and manipulation or emotional abuse is absent.

Developing the ability to identify signs of a healthy relationship involves a deep sense of self-awareness. It's about knowing your needs, understanding your boundaries, and being able to communicate them effectively. Recognizing a healthy relationship also means understanding that you deserve to be in a space where you are respected, valued, and your emotional needs are met.

Part of this process is learning. Reflecting on what went wrong in the toxic relationship can provide valuable insights into what you seek in future connections. It's also about being open to experiencing relationships that bring joy, support, and mutual growth, and not just those that feel familiar.

Developing Emotional Resilience

Another critical aspect of moving forward is developing emotional resilience. This resilience is the ability to recover from difficulties, adapt to change, and keep going in the face of adversity. Emotional resilience is what helps you navigate future challenges with a sense of strength and flexibility.

Building emotional resilience can involve a variety of practices. Mindfulness, for instance, helps you stay grounded and present, managing stress more effectively. Engaging in activities that bring you joy and fulfillment also nurtures your emotional strength. Surrounding yourself with a supportive community, whether it's friends, family, or support groups, can provide a sense of belonging and strength.

Embracing a Future of Healing and Growth

The journey of healing and recovery from a toxic relationship culminates in a powerful transformation. It's a path that intertwines the renewal of self-trust, the cultivation of healthy relationships, and the development of emotional resilience. Each of these elements contributes to rebuilding a life marked by emotional well-being and strength.

Reclaiming trust in oneself lays the foundation for this transformation. It's about rekindling faith in your judgment and instincts, a process that restores confidence and empowers decision-making. Recognizing and engaging in healthy relationships then becomes a reflection of this renewed self-trust. It involves discerning relationships that are nurturing and supportive, ones that encourage growth and mutual respect.

Simultaneously, developing emotional resilience equips you to face future challenges with a newfound strength and flexibility. This resilience, forged through mindfulness, positive self-engagement, and supportive networks, becomes your shield against the adversities that life may present. It's about adapting to change and emerging stronger from each challenge.

This multifaceted journey, while demanding patience and persistence, paves the way towards a future filled with healthier relationships and a deeper understanding of oneself. It's a testament to the human spirit's ability to transform past pain into resilience and renewal. The scars from the toxic relationship may remain as reminders of what you have overcome, but they also signify your capacity for growth, strength, and the promise of a more fulfilling, authentic existence.

As you walk this path of healing and recovery, remember that each step is a stride towards a brighter, more empowered future. It's a journey not just of recovery but of rediscovering and reclaiming a life defined by self-respect, joy, and emotional balance.

Chapter 8:

Setting Boundaries and Asserting Yourself

You can leave a toxic relationship, but if you don't heal what attracted you to them, you will meet them again. The same demon, just in a different person. —The Minds Journal

The journey towards healthy and fulfilling relationships often hinges on our ability to set and maintain clear boundaries. This chapter delves into the critical importance of boundary-setting in relationships, offering insights and strategies for assertive communication and self-advocacy. Boundaries are not just protective barriers; they are affirmations of our self-respect, autonomy, and the values we wish to uphold in our interactions with others. By learning to articulate and enforce these boundaries, we lay the groundwork for relationships based on mutual respect and understanding.

Consider the story of Amelia, a go-to person in her office, known for her reliability and approachability. However, working with Candace, a manipulative coworker, strained Amelia's well-being and professional relationships. Amelia's journey to reclaim her space and peace of mind at work exemplifies the transformative power of setting boundaries.

Amelia took the first step by addressing Candace's behavior assertively, calmly expressing her discomfort, and refusing to accept any further manipulative tactics. She employed "I" statements such as "I feel uncomfortable when you take credit for my work," effectively communicating her feelings without assigning blame. Amelia also established non-negotiable limits, clarifying that her time and energy were valuable and not to be encroached upon.

This shift towards assertiveness and self-advocacy marked a significant turning point for Amelia. Her newfound assertiveness began reshaping the dynamics at her workplace. What had once been an environment of manipulation and disrespect gradually transformed into one of respect and professionalism. Amelia's experience is a testament to the fact that setting boundaries is an empowering act of self-care, essential for maintaining one's mental and emotional well-being.

In this chapter, we will explore various facets of setting boundaries and asserting oneself. We will provide strategies to help you identify your personal boundaries, communicate them effectively, and maintain them in the face of challenges. Through this process, you will learn not just to protect yourself from being taken advantage of, but also to foster healthier, more balanced relationships in all areas of your life.

Understanding the Role of Boundaries

The process of setting boundaries and asserting oneself is pivotal in navigating life post-toxic relationships. This journey begins with a profound understanding of the role of personal boundaries, which act as crucial guidelines in our interactions, defining what is acceptable and what isn't in our relationships. Boundaries are the emotional, physical, and psychological limits we set to protect our well-being and respect our individuality within various relationships. They are vital because they provide a framework within which we can interact with others in a healthy, respectful manner. Boundaries enable us to protect ourselves from being manipulated, exploited, or emotionally harmed, thus preserving our sense of self and personal integrity.

More than just barriers to keep others at bay, boundaries reflect self-awareness and an acknowledgment of our own limits. They help delineate our personal space, beliefs, and needs, allowing for emotional intimacy and genuine connections while safeguarding our individuality. Healthy boundaries are not rigid or static; they evolve as we grow and as our circumstances change, demonstrating flexibility and adaptability.

Implementing healthy boundaries brings many benefits to our relationships. They foster respect and autonomy, enabling us to maintain control over our decisions and actions, and contribute to a sense of empowerment. In romantic relationships, for instance, having clear boundaries about personal space or communication styles fosters mutual respect and understanding.

In conflict resolution, healthy boundaries create a framework that aids in addressing disagreements constructively. When boundaries are clear, issues can be discussed without misunderstanding or overstepping each other's limits. In professional settings, establishing boundaries around workload and responsibilities can lead to more effective collaboration and conflict management.

Boundaries are essential for emotional well-being, serving as a defense mechanism against emotional manipulation and abuse. They affirm our right to emotional safety and well-being, protecting us from vulnerabilities being exploited. Additionally, when boundaries are respected, it builds trust in the relationship, with each party feeling confident that their limits will be honored, fostering a safe environment. This trust lays the foundation for deeper, more meaningful connections.

Recognizing when boundaries have been crossed is also crucial for maintaining healthy relationships. Violations can range from subtle intrusions, like unsolicited advice, to more overt breaches, such as disrespecting personal space or emotional manipulation. These violations can lead to feelings of resentment, discomfort, and a breakdown in trust, undermining the foundation of respect and safety that healthy relationships are built upon.

Addressing boundary violations involves assertiveness and constructive communication. It may mean reiterating the boundary, explaining its importance, and discussing the consequences of continued breaches. For example, if a family member repeatedly crosses a boundary by offering unsolicited opinions on personal matters, a candid conversation about respecting personal space and privacy may be necessary.

Understanding and implementing personal boundaries is a key step in healing from toxic relationships and building a future with healthier, more respectful interactions. This chapter will explore further strategies and insights essential for setting boundaries and asserting oneself effectively.

Strategies for Setting and Communicating Boundaries

The foundation of healthy interactions lies in setting personal boundaries. This task, while crucial, can often present challenges. To begin, it's important to understand your own needs, values, and limitations. Reflecting on past experiences helps in determining your comfort levels with various behaviors. For example, you might consider the extent of personal information you're willing to share in the workplace or your preferences regarding physical contact in social settings.

Once you've identified your boundaries, the next step is to articulate them clearly to others. This communication should be direct and unambiguous, to avoid misunderstandings. Say, for example, you need a quiet environment to work effectively.

Communicating this need clearly and firmly to your colleagues or family is essential.

Maintaining consistency in enforcing your boundaries is equally critical. Inconsistencies or bending under pressure can send mixed signals, undermining the seriousness with which others take your boundaries. By maintaining consistency, you not only reinforce your boundaries but set a standard for the respect you desire from others.

Assertive Communication

Assertive communication is a vital tool in setting and maintaining boundaries. It enables you to express your needs and limits respectfully and confidently. When conveying your needs, use "I" statements to express your feelings and preferences. This approach shifts the focus from accusing others to expressing your own needs. For instance, instead of saying, "You always call me at inconvenient times," try, "I feel overwhelmed when I receive calls during my work hours. Can we schedule a time that works for both of us?"

While being assertive, it's also important to stay respectful and empathetic. Acknowledge the other person's feelings and perspective but remain firm on your boundaries. If someone disregards your boundaries, address the violation directly and calmly, explaining why your boundaries are important and discussing potential consequences if they continue to be disregarded.

Handling Resistance and Pushback

When you introduce new boundaries, especially in established relationships, resistance is common. It's crucial to stay firm and confident in the face of this resistance. Reaffirm your boundaries and explain their importance to you. Remember, not giving in to pressure is essential for setting a precedent in future interactions.

Be prepared for the dynamics of the relationship to change. Some individuals might react negatively to new boundaries, especially if they are accustomed to a different dynamic. Keep communication open and discuss how these changes are mutually beneficial.

Managing negative reactions like anger or disappointment is also part of this process. Not everyone will respond positively to your boundaries, but it's important to prioritize your well-being and not feel guilty about setting healthy limits.

Navigating Challenging Conversations

Managing conflicts effectively is a key component of healthy relationships, requiring a blend of clear communication, understanding, and a commitment to collaborative problem-solving.

Assertiveness in Communication

When addressing conflicts, assertiveness is paramount. It involves expressing your thoughts and needs clearly while also respecting the perspectives of others. For instance, if a family decision doesn't sit well with you, it's crucial to convey your standpoint and offer alternatives, emphasizing the issue at hand rather than assigning blame (Sutton, 2020).

In managing disagreements, several strategies can be beneficial. Active listening is crucial; it involves fully grasping the other person's point of view, both in words and emotions. Keeping a level head and focusing on the matter at hand is also essential, as heightened emotions can further complicate conflicts (Segal et al., 2019). Seeking collaborative solutions that accommodate everyone's needs and boundaries is the goal, and it may involve compromise or creative approaches to problem-solving (Gupta, 2023).

The Art of Empathetic Listening

Empathetic listening is central to understanding others' needs and facilitating successful interactions. It's about fully engaging with the speaker, showing that you value their input. Techniques for effective listening include giving complete attention, paraphrasing or summarizing their words to ensure understanding, and employing non-verbal gestures, such as nodding or maintaining eye contact, to demonstrate engagement. Creating an atmosphere conducive to open, honest communication is also important, where everyone feels secure to share their thoughts and feelings (Segal et al., 2019).

Building Mutual Respect through Compromise

In any relationship, mutual respect and the ability to compromise are vital for sustaining harmony. Advocating for your needs while respecting others' boundaries promotes mutual understanding (Richer, 2021). Finding compromises that suit all parties is about adjusting boundaries or finding middle ground that respects everyone's comfort zones (Gupta, 2023). This requires a balance between individual needs and collective considerations, calling for flexibility and empathy.

In sum, mastering difficult dialogues in relationships is about effectively combining assertive communication with empathetic listening and a readiness to find middle ground. These skills are crucial for resolving conflicts in a way that strengthens relationships, building trust and deepening connections.

Nurturing Empowerment through Boundaries and Communication

As we conclude this chapter, the essence of empowerment through setting boundaries and assertive communication becomes clear. These crucial skills, applicable across personal and professional realms, help to forge healthier, more balanced relationships.

Setting personal boundaries goes beyond mere refusals; it is a profound act of self-care and self-respect. These boundaries act as protective barriers for our emotional and mental well-being, enabling us to cultivate relationships that are respectful, nurturing, and empowering. They allow us to maintain our individuality and promote an environment of mutual respect.

Assertive communication emerges as a powerful tool for self-empowerment. It's not just about being heard; it's about expressing needs and feelings confidently and respectfully. This skill boosts self-assurance and respect, equipping us to tackle even challenging conversations with grace and poise. Assertiveness, rooted in respect and firmness, ensures that our voices are acknowledged and our needs addressed.

Empathetic listening and understanding others' perspectives are crucial for fostering effective communication. They deepen our connections and foster relationships based on trust and mutual understanding. Engaging in dialogues that are both solution-oriented and empathetic enriches our interactions and strengthens our bonds.

Chapter 9:

Moving Forward and Thriving Beyond Toxic Relationships

Forgive others not because they deserve forgiveness, but because you deserve peace. —Jonathan Lockwood Huielt

This chapter is more than just a guide to emerging from the shadows of past hurts; it's a blueprint for building a future rich in growth, self-awareness, and unlimited potential. We anchor our narrative in the transformative story of Justin, whose journey of forgiving his mother illustrates the essence of moving forward. His decision, centered less on excusing the pain inflicted and more on freeing himself from the bitterness that anchored him to a stagnant past, marked the start of an ascent into a life redefined by personal growth and emotional healing. Justin's story exemplifies the impact of releasing resentment, a necessary step to thrive in both personal and professional realms.

As we traverse this chapter, we dissect the intricate processes of acceptance, letting go, and achieving closure—vital elements in shedding the remnants of toxic relationships. We explore the concept of radical acceptance, equipping you with the tools to embrace past experiences without letting them overshadow your present and future. We unravel the art of letting go, a skill that demands courage and grace, illustrating how detaching from past traumas can open the door to emotional freedom and a renewed sense of self.

The journey beyond toxic relationships is complex and deeply personal. It calls for acknowledging the past's impact while firmly stepping towards a future filled with possibilities. Our exploration transcends mere survival; it's about thriving in the aftermath, flourishing in uncharted territories of self-discovery, and embracing personal growth as a lifelong journey.

This chapter is an invitation to join us on this transformative journey. We delve into stories like Justin's, showcasing the resilience and strength required to navigate and overcome past toxicities. This exploration is a vital step towards empowerment, healing, and reclaiming your narrative.

In this journey, understanding how to move forward from toxic relationships also involves reclaiming your autonomy and truth. It's about recognizing when your reality is being distorted and learning to firmly anchor in your own experiences and perceptions. We embark on this path of enlightenment, understanding, and self-empowerment, where each step is a move towards reclaiming your peace, joy, and future.

Acceptance and Letting Go

Acceptance is a transformative tool for healing. It's about acknowledging the past and its pain, thus freeing yourself from the emotional burdens of resentment and regret (Taitz, 2021). Embracing the past is a choice to prioritize emotional health over stagnation. When you accept the pain and damage caused, you no longer carry the weight of bitterness, anger, or regret, allowing you to move forward with a lighter heart and mind (Cook, 2020).

Practicing radical acceptance involves mindfulness and self-compassion, helping you become aware of and accept your feelings related to the past without judgment (Floyd, 2019). Journaling and self-reflection are valuable for processing and coming to terms with these emotions, gaining insights into your resilience. Seeking support and therapy can guide you through this acceptance process, providing tools for managing the emotional aftermath of toxic relationships (Rostorfer, 2017). It's about understanding that the past is unchangeable and focusing on shaping your future (*Need for Closure*, n.d.).

The Art of Letting Go

Letting go is pivotal in moving forward from toxic relationships. It's about releasing emotional attachments to the past and focusing on the future. This intentional decision frees you from the past's grip (Van Dyke, 2021).

Strategies for releasing emotional attachments include forgiveness, which is not about condoning harmful behavior but about freeing yourself from emotional burdens. Mindfulness and present-centered living help you embrace the present's beauty and opportunities. Symbolic acts, like writing and releasing a letter to the person or relationship you need to let go of, can be cathartic (Ramsden, 2018). Focusing on a positive vision for your future helps shift focus from what you're leaving behind to what you're moving toward (Hardy, 2023).

Closure and Moving On

Closure is essential in moving on from toxic relationships. It involves finding a sense of finality with the past and opening the door to new beginnings. Emotional expression, whether through journaling, therapy, or discussions, helps process and release feelings related to the toxic relationship. Recognizing the relationship's harmful nature helps detach from lingering feelings of guilt, blame, or responsibility. Engaging in acts of closure, like returning or disposing of items that remind you of the relationship, can be powerful. Establishing boundaries with the person you're moving on from prevents further emotional entanglement.

Closure brings psychological freedom, allowing you to embark on new paths. Self-forgiveness, integral to this process, involves releasing self-blame and recognizing your right to happiness and healthy relationships (Germer & Neff, 2014).

The art of compromise and fostering mutual respect are also pivotal to maintain harmony in relationships. Balancing our needs with those of others requires flexibility, understanding, and sometimes creative problem-solving. This balance is crucial for creating relationships that are cooperative and mutually fulfilling.

As these skills evolve with our growth and experiences, they reflect our deepening understanding of ourselves and our relationships. This continuous adaptation enhances our interactions and contributes positively to our overall well-being.

The journey toward healthier relationships is ongoing. With the strategies and knowledge, we are better prepared to navigate this path. The practices of setting boundaries and assertive communication are not just strategies but acts of self-empowerment, leading us towards more fulfilling and respectful relationships. They are reminders of our strength, resilience, and capacity for growth and renewal in our interpersonal connections.

Personal Growth and Self-Discovery

Emerging from toxic relationships often marks the beginning of profound personal growth and self-improvement. This journey offers invaluable opportunities for building resilience, enhancing self-awareness, and developing empathy and more robust relationship skills.

Surviving and overcoming toxic relationships often instills resilience and strength, underscoring your capability to face challenges and come out stronger. These experiences can also be immensely educational, providing insights into your personal needs, boundaries, and values, which become the foundation for future informed choices. Having experienced toxicity firsthand, you may develop greater empathy and compassion, useful in supporting others facing similar challenges. This journey also serves as a platform for honing healthier relationship skills, fostering positive changes in your future interactions.

Several strategies can aid in setting personal development goals. Journaling is a potent tool for self-reflection, helping you to crystallize your experiences and identify areas for growth, such as assertive communication or setting boundaries. Therapeutic support can also play a significant role in identifying and achieving personal development goals. Engaging in educational pursuits like workshops and seminars can provide further insights and strategies for self-improvement, while leaning on your support network can offer encouragement and accountability (Rostorfer, 2017).

Remember, personal growth is an ongoing, transformative journey. Embrace change and evolution, understanding that setbacks are opportunities to learn and adapt. Celebrate your achievements and practice self-compassion as you progress on this path.

Cultivating Self-Discovery

Self-discovery is about delving deep into understanding yourself, your values, passions, and aspirations. This transformative process begins with introspection, examining your thoughts, emotions, and experiences to gain insight into who you are. Reflecting on your experiences in toxic relationships can be particularly enlightening, shedding light on how these experiences have shaped your values and desires.

Exploring your passions and interests is an exciting part of self-discovery. Identify what excites you and brings joy, as these passions can reveal much about your true self. Embracing self-acceptance is also vital, acknowledging all aspects of yourself, including those you previously considered flaws or weaknesses.

Several techniques can help explore your values, passions, and aspirations. Journaling is an effective way to delve into your thoughts and feelings related to your values and dreams. Mindfulness and meditation practices can help connect you with your inner self. Seeking new experiences and stepping outside your comfort zone can uncover unknown passions and interests. Working with a therapist specializing in self-discovery and personal growth can provide valuable guidance (Perry, 2023).

Self-discovery steers you toward a fulfilling and purposeful life. It involves aligning your life choices with your values for a sense of fulfillment and purpose. Pursuing your passions leads to a profound sense of meaning and happiness. Gaining clarity on who you are and what you want sets the stage for clear goals and purposeful actions. A better understanding of yourself also enhances your ability to communicate needs and boundaries, leading to healthier relationships.

In summary, self-discovery encompasses introspection, reflection, acceptance, and exploration of your values, passions, and aspirations. Techniques such as journaling, mindfulness, new experiences, and therapeutic guidance can facilitate this journey, leading to a life characterized by value alignment, passion-driven experiences, clarity of purpose, and improved relationships.

Building Resilience and Emotional Strength

Emotional resilience is not just about recovering from past hardships; it's about strengthening your ability to navigate future challenges with a positive and adaptive mindset. This resilience is integral in recovering from the emotional upheaval caused by toxic relationships, aiding in rebuilding self-confidence and regaining a sense of self-worth. It involves seeing challenges as opportunities for growth and empowerment, allowing you to control your emotional responses rather than being controlled by them.

To enhance emotional resilience, several practices can be beneficial. Mindfulness techniques, such as meditation and deep breathing, help in regulating emotions and staying present in the moment. Emotional regulation skills are essential for managing stress healthily and can be developed through practices like deep breathing during times of stress. Problem-solving skills also play a crucial role in addressing challenges effectively, reducing overall stress. A strong support network is invaluable in providing emotional backing and guidance during tough times.

Fostering resilience also involves maintaining a positive outlook and being adaptable in the face of adversity. This includes engaging in positive self-talk, being flexible with your goals and strategies, setting realistic goals, and engaging in self-care activities like exercise and relaxation techniques. These practices not only aid in coping with stress but also contribute to your overall mental and emotional well-being.

Support networks are a vital component in building emotional strength. They provide a sense of emotional validation, understanding, and motivation. Sharing your feelings with trusted individuals can ease emotional distress and reduce the sense of isolation often caused by toxic relationships. Empathetic listening from friends and family offers comfort and understanding, while words of affirmation can motivate and inspire positive actions. Nurturing these relationships involves open communication, respecting each other's boundaries, spending quality time together, and offering mutual support.

Professional guidance from therapists can also offer specialized expertise in navigating the emotional complexities post-toxic relationships. Peer support groups offer shared experiences and valuable advice, and learning to ask for help when needed is an important aspect of self-care. Clearly communicating your needs within your support network is self-advocacy that reinforces your emotional resilience.

In parallel, self-compassion and self-care are indispensable for maintaining emotional strength. They provide the emotional nourishment to recover from the exhaustion caused by toxic relationships and are key to building resilience. Prioritizing self-care reduces stress levels and fosters emotional well-being. Self-compassion involves treating yourself with kindness and understanding, recognizing that setbacks are opportunities for growth, and maintaining a supportive inner dialogue.

Cultivating emotional resilience following toxic relationships entails being mindful, regulating emotions, developing problem-solving capabilities, and seeking support from networks. It's about cultivating a mindset that embraces change, seeks growth, and finds strength in adversity. Support networks provide essential emotional strength, and self-compassion and self-care practices underpin the journey towards emotional resilience. Together, these elements empower you to face future challenges with determination and a positive outlook, transforming past pain into a catalyst for personal growth and emotional strength.

Embracing a Thriving Future

This journey marks not just a departure from past adversities, but an embrace of a future vibrant with possibilities and fulfillment.

At the heart of thriving lies emotional freedom, a liberating experience where you can authentically feel and express your emotions, unshackled from past constraints. This newfound freedom paves the way for improved mental health, reduced stress, and a surge in happiness. It's reclaiming your identity, rediscovering passions, interests, and values that might have been dimmed by previous toxic experiences. Thriving cultivates the ground for fostering healthy relationships, characterized by mutual respect, trust, and love. Moreover, it's an opportunity to engage in personal growth, setting new goals, acquiring skills, and evolving continually.

A vital component of this thriving future is the development of healthy, fulfilling connections. This involves practicing open and honest communication, where sharing feelings and needs becomes a two-way street marked by understanding and receptiveness. Defining and communicating boundaries clearly is crucial to ensure mutual respect and understanding in these connections. The cultivation of empathy deepens these bonds, promoting emotional intimacy and understanding. Building connections with individuals who share similar interests and values leads to relationships that are both meaningful and supportive.

The transformative journey of thriving is akin to a new beginning, a chance to rewrite your narrative with healing and resilience as its core themes. It's about seizing opportunities to explore new possibilities, taking risks, and indulging in self-love, a blend of self-compassion, acceptance, and celebration of your uniqueness.

Setting and pursuing goals becomes an integral aspect of this thriving life. Goals infuse life with direction and purpose, serving as motivators and markers of progress. They are catalysts for personal growth, pushing you to learn and venture beyond your comfort zone. Effective goal-setting involves defining clear, achievable objectives, breaking them into smaller, manageable steps, and regularly reviewing and adjusting these goals. Sharing these goals with someone who can offer support and accountability adds a layer of motivation and encouragement.

The journey of thriving is continuous, woven with challenges and opportunities for growth and happiness. Embracing challenges with resilience, practicing gratitude for the present moment, and maintaining an optimistic outlook are key elements of this journey. Thriving involves nurturing positive qualities such as mindfulness to stay present, fostering gratitude for life's blessings, engaging in positive self-talk, and leaning on your support network for guidance and motivation.

In this ongoing journey, recognizing the need for adaptability and continual growth is paramount. Thriving isn't a static state but a dynamic process of embracing change, learning, and evolving into a happier, more fulfilled self. It's a journey that continually unfolds, offering endless opportunities for learning, adapting, and evolving into your best self.

Thriving after a toxic relationship is about embracing a future replete with emotional freedom, personal growth, and the joy of healthy relationships. It's a journey defined by pursuing goals, facing challenges with resilience, and prioritizing personal well-being and fulfillment.

Section 3:

Empowerment

Chapter 10:

Preventing and Breaking the Cycle of Toxic Relationships

I've had a few semi-toxic relationships, but it's not what I'm looking for when I'm seeing someone. —Taylor Swift

Herer, we embark on an empowering journey, guiding us away from the cycle of toxic relationships and towards the development of healthier, more fulfilling connections. Central to this journey is the story of Lucy, who, after escaping a toxic marriage, unwittingly found herself drawn into a similar relationship. Her story, however, transforms from a cycle of despair to one of enlightenment and change. Lucy's realization of her pattern of toxic relationships catalyzed a transformative journey of self-discovery and healing, highlighting the crucial role of self-reflection and awareness in breaking free from unhealthy relationship cycles.

Self-Reflection and Awareness

Self-reflection stands as a beacon in the journey away from toxic relationships, serving as a critical tool for understanding and reshaping one's relationship patterns. It involves deep introspection, where individuals examine their thoughts, emotions, and behaviors to unravel the intricacies of their past relational experiences. Techniques such as journaling, meditation, and seeking feedback help in identifying emotional patterns, clarifying values, and understanding personal needs and boundaries. This process is vital in recognizing and preventing the repetition of toxic relationships, fostering personal growth, and setting the stage for relationships based on mutual respect and understanding.

Lucy's journey through self-reflection illustrates how identifying detrimental patterns and vulnerabilities is a catalyst for positive change. This process equips us with the insights needed to choose healthier relationship dynamics that align with their personal values and boundaries. Exploring vulnerabilities, such as emotional wounds and insecurities, becomes a proactive step in guarding against toxic relationships. Understanding past traumas and their influence on relationship choices illuminates the reasons behind repetitive, unhealthy patterns, offering a pathway for change.

Embracing vulnerabilities with kindness and compassion is an empowering aspect of this journey. It involves understanding that addressing these vulnerabilities head-on equips individuals with the knowledge and tools to avert potentially toxic relationships. Self-reflection and awareness thus become cornerstones in the journey towards healthier relational waters.

Lucy's story and the insights in this chapter underscore the power of self-reflection and awareness when breaking free from these dynamics. They highlight the journey of transforming understanding into action, leading to choices that align with one's true values, needs, and boundaries. This journey is not just about moving away from negative experiences; it's about progressing towards a life that is enriching and fulfilling, grounded in self-awareness and empowerment.

Building Self-Esteem and Self-Worth

The next pivotal step in our journey, much like Lucy's, Chris's, and Alex's experiences, is the rebuilding of self-esteem and self-worth. This phase is crucial for healing and empowerment, especially after exiting toxic relationships. It is akin to nurturing a garden back to life after a storm, where regaining self-confidence and re-establishing a sense of self become imperative.

Rebuilding Self-Esteem

Rebuilding self-esteem is essential for recovering from the emotional damage inflicted by toxic relationships. It empowers individuals to value their own needs, make empowered choices, and refuse to settle for anything less than they deserve. A healthy sense of self-esteem acts as a barrier against the recurrence of toxic relationships, ensuring individuals don't fall back into familiar, harmful patterns. It fosters awareness of one's worth, enabling the establishment of firm boundaries and guiding individuals towards relationships characterized by mutual respect and fulfillment.

Chris's transformation exemplifies this journey. After emerging from a toxic relationship, they engaged in therapy, assertiveness training, and dedicated self-care practices. This process gradually restored Chris's sense of self-worth, leading them to make choices more aligned with their values and needs and paving the way for healthier, more respectful relationships.

Cultivating Self-Compassion

Cultivating self-compassion is a vital component of the healing process. It involves extending kindness and understanding to oneself, acknowledging personal pain, and treating it with empathy. Self-compassion promotes self-worth and contributes significantly to emotional well-being.

Practicing self-compassion and self-love involves responding to self-criticism with kindness, practicing mindfulness to remain present and non-judgmental towards one's emotional state, and recognizing that suffering is a part of the human experience. This approach not only bolsters self-esteem but also contributes to the health of future relationships, enabling individuals to communicate their needs effectively and seek partners who offer respect and kindness.

Alex's journey post-toxic relationship showcases the power of self-compassion. Through practices like self-kindness, mindfulness, and embracing their shared humanity, Alex not only healed from past hurts but also built the foundation for healthier future relationships.

This journey is not just about recovery; it's about empowerment and the creation of a future where relationships uplift and support, reflecting true love and respect.

Cultivating Healthy Relationships

Cultivating healthy relationships is crucial for healing and fulfillment after toxic experiences. This process, as exemplified in the stories of Mark, Sarah, and Lisa, involves embracing relationships characterized by open communication, mutual respect, trust, and transparency. These elements are the building blocks for nurturing personal growth and happiness in any relationship.

Understanding one's own values, needs, and boundaries is the first step in identifying and fostering healthy relationships. This self-awareness is a compass guiding individuals towards connections that resonate with their core beliefs and emotional well-being. Mark's journey post-toxic relationship is a prime example of this. By prioritizing self-awareness, effective communication, and mutual respect, he found a partner who shared his values, leading to a relationship where open communication and trust flourished.

Effective communication and mutual respect are the cornerstones of any healthy relationship. They are essential for resolving conflicts and maintaining a strong connection. These practices allow partners to understand each other's needs and address concerns in ways that build rather than break the bond. Mutual respect is about valuing each other's boundaries, values, and individuality, creating a nurturing and respectful environment.

Approaching new relationships with optimism and an understanding that past experiences don't dictate future happiness is crucial. Healthy relationships contribute significantly to personal growth and emotional well-being. They encourage individuals to maintain healthy boundaries and self-respect, ensuring that they enter relationships that honor their emotional safety and self-worth.

Navigating conflict and resolution healthily is vital for sustaining positive relationships. Healthy conflict resolution involves addressing disagreements constructively and finding solutions that benefit all parties involved. This approach prevents resentment and fosters empathy and understanding. Techniques like active listening, using "I" statements, and seeking compromise play a crucial role in this process. Sarah and Lisa's transformation in their friendship illustrates the power of healthy conflict resolution. By embracing open communication and active listening, they were able to transform their friendship into a healthier, more constructive relationship.

Finally, recognizing and avoiding recurring patterns of toxicity is an ongoing process. It involves regular self-reflection, seeking professional help when needed, and setting healthy boundaries. This proactive approach helps individuals avoid falling back into familiar, harmful relationship patterns, paving the way for healthier future connections.

Nurturing connections is a testament to the resilience and strength inherent in individuals. It's about thriving in relationships that uplift and support, reflecting the true essence of love and respect. This path involves understanding one's values, embracing effective communication, fostering mutual respect, and actively working to prevent the recurrence of toxic patterns. It's a transformative process that leads not just to recovery, but to a richer, more fulfilling relational experience.

As we transition to the next chapter, we carry forward the insights and lessons learned from cultivating healthy relationships. This builds upon the foundations laid in breaking free from toxic dynamics and focuses on sustaining and enhancing the journey towards personal empowerment and emotional wellness. It will review strategies for ongoing self-improvement, embracing life's challenges as opportunities for growth, and maintaining a balanced and fulfilling life. The journey ahead is one of continuous exploration, reflection, and growth, a path that leads not only to healing but to a future replete with potential and well-being.

Chapter 11:

Continuing Your Journey to Personal Growth and Well-Being

Life becomes easier when you learn to accept an apology you never got.
—Robert Brault

Our focus now moves beyond recovery, prioritizing flourishing after adversity and creating a fulfilling, happy life.

Phil's story serves as a beacon on this path. His journey from the remnants of a toxic relationship to a life marked by self-improvement and well-being mirrors the transformative process we aim to explore. Phil's experience of reconnecting with friends, rekindling old passions, and engaging in therapy to heal emotional wounds illustrates the multifaceted nature of this journey. His dedication to self-care, both mentally and physically, and the shift from a critical inner voice to one of self-compassion and encouragement, exemplifies the profound impact and importance of personal growth and well-being.

I want us to review some practical and empowering strategies to maintain and enhance the positive changes made in the healing process. The focus is on practices such as self-reflection and mindfulness, which are pivotal in fostering self-awareness and emotional balance. We will also address coping with setbacks and challenges, underscoring the significance of resilience, adaptability, and seeking support in times of difficulty.

We will explore the rewarding process of embracing your journey. This part of the chapter will highlight the ongoing benefits of well-being, the cultivation of resilience, and the joy of thriving in a future brimming with personal growth and happiness.

It's about embracing life's complexities, transforming each day into an opportunity for growth, learning, and joy. This chapter is a celebration of continuous self-improvement, a testament to the enduring nature of personal development, and an invitation to embrace a future filled with potential and well-being.

Cultivating Self-Reflection and Mindfulness

Self-reflection and mindfulness stand as pillars of personal growth and well-being. These practices, crucial for individuals like Phil and Sarah, facilitate a deeper understanding of oneself, fostering emotional healing and self-awareness.

Self-reflection helps to build this self-awareness, allowing individuals to gain insights into their emotional landscapes and behaviors. Understanding the impact of past experiences is crucial for making informed decisions (Allo Health, 2023). By identifying patterns in relationships and emotional responses, individuals can break cycles of toxicity and foster healthier choices in the future. Techniques like journaling, meditation, and regular self-check-ins can provide clarity on emotional triggers and complex feelings.

Mindfulness complements self-reflection by nurturing an acute awareness of internal experiences. It aids in understanding emotional responses and triggers, which is crucial for healing and growth (Eric, n.d.). Practices such as meditation and deep breathing exercises effectively reduce emotional turmoil and promote calm (*Peer Support Workers for Those in Recovery*, 2017). Regular mindfulness practices like meditation, mindful eating, and deep breathing exercises helped Mark manage stress, improve emotional regulation, and embrace a more mindful and balanced lifestyle.

Setting personal growth goals is also vital in the recovery journey. These goals aid in healing from emotional wounds and encourage a positive forward trajectory. By identifying core values and beliefs, individuals can align their goals with personal priorities. Sarah's strategic setting of personal growth goals, focusing on self-esteem and emotional resilience, marked significant strides in her emotional well-being (*Learn Something Series: Empathy, Listening, & Vulnerability*, n.d.).

Coping with Setbacks and Challenges

Setbacks are not only inevitable but an essential part of personal growth. Instead of hurdles, these setbacks are steppingstones towards self-understanding and resilience.

When individuals like John, who emerged from a toxic work environment, face setbacks reminiscent of past adversities, they can approach these challenges with a renewed perspective. Instead of viewing setbacks as failures, embracing them with self-compassion and understanding their inherent value in the growth process can transform these experiences into powerful lessons.

The art of coping with setbacks involves a blend of self-reflection, open communication with a support network, and a shift in mindset. It's about acknowledging the normalcy of these experiences in the healing journey and using them as a catalyst for further development (VibewithAsia, 2023). Sharing struggles with trusted friends or therapists can provide not only a sense of relief but also a different perspective that aids in navigating these challenges more effectively.

Adaptability plays a crucial role in this process. It's about viewing changes and challenges not as obstacles but as opportunities for growth and learning. For instance, James' story of turning an unexpected job loss into a chance for a fulfilling new career is a prime example of adaptability in action. His ability to embrace change, build resilience, and remain flexible in his approach exemplified how adaptability is key to overcoming life's challenges and fostering well-being.

Maintaining a positive outlook is equally important. It involves reframing setbacks as growth opportunities and setting realistic goals to maintain a sense of progress and direction. Regular self-reflection helps to keep track of personal growth, and adjusting strategies as needed ensures that setbacks become valuable lessons rather than impediments (National Alliance on Mental Illness, 2020).

This is an integral part of healing from toxic relationships. It's a process that fosters resilience, adaptability, and a positive outlook, all of which are crucial for ongoing personal growth and well-being. By embracing this journey with self-compassion, seeking support, and cultivating a mindset of growth and flexibility, individuals can turn their experiences into powerful catalysts for transformation and empowerment.

Embracing Your Journey

As this chapter draws to a close, it encapsulates the essence of an ongoing journey toward personal growth and well-being—a journey that extends beyond merely overcoming past adversities to flourishing in their aftermath. This path, illuminated by individuals like Phil and Sarah, underscores the significance of continual self-improvement, resilience, and the cultivation of nurturing relationships as cornerstones for a thriving life.

Embarking on this journey demands a deep commitment to self-reflection and mindfulness. It's about persistently examining and understanding one's inner world—thoughts, emotions, and behaviors—to foster a profound self-awareness that guides future decisions and interactions. Techniques like journaling, meditation, and regular self-evaluations, exemplified in Sarah's transformative journey, play crucial roles in maintaining this introspective practice. They enable individuals to track their progress, recognize their growth milestones, and continually realign themselves with their evolving values and aspirations.

Integral to this journey is the development and maintenance of emotional resilience. This resilience isn't just about recovering from setbacks, but about transforming them into opportunities for growth and learning. It involves cultivating a mindset where challenges are seen as steppingstones rather than obstacles. Practices such as positive self-talk, emotional regulation through mindfulness, and adaptive problem-solving are pivotal in building this resilience. Nurturing a supportive network that includes friends, family, and professionals provides a crucial emotional anchor, offering diverse perspectives and emotional support in times of need.

The journey towards well-being is marked by the pursuit of thriving, fostering relationships that support personal growth, setting meaningful goals, and embracing life's myriad opportunities with optimism and openness. It's about shaping a future where relationships are grounded in mutual respect and communication, mirroring the positive changes one has cultivated within. This pursuit of a thriving life is not static; it's an ongoing process of adaptation and growth, as seen in the stories of Mark and Emily, who embraced new goals and relationships with an open heart and a forward-looking mindset.

As we move from embracing the journey of personal growth and well-being, the focus shifts to sustaining and enhancing these positive changes. The upcoming chapter aims to provide further insights and strategies for continuing this path of self-discovery and development, ensuring that the journey towards a fulfilling and balanced life is not just a temporary sojourn but a lifelong commitment to growth, learning, and joy.

Chapter 12:

Supporting Others in Toxic Relationships

Good friends help you find important things when you have lost them…
things like your smile, your hope and your courage.
—Doe Zantamata

In the tapestry of human relationships, the threads of empathy, support, and empowerment are intertwined, forming the fabric of healing and transformation. This chapter delves into the art of supporting those entangled in challenging relationships, a journey that calls for patience, understanding, and active engagement.

The story of Marie and Joanna serves as a beacon, illustrating how empathy can be a sanctuary for those struggling. Empathy goes beyond mere listening; it's about feeling with someone, understanding their pain, and acknowledging their experiences. This empathetic connection opens the doors to trust and honest communication, which are essential in guiding someone towards recognizing their self-worth and considering change.

This chapter provides a roadmap for readers on how to be a source of strength and guidance for those entangled in toxic relationships. It will offer a combination of personal narratives, expert insights, and practical advice to equip readers with the tools to effectively support others.

We aim to empower you with strategies for offering support, understanding, and empowerment. It explores the nuances of providing empathetic support, sharing resources, and fostering an environment where individuals feel empowered to make informed decisions and reclaim their autonomy. The goal is to demonstrate how, through empathy and empowerment, one can be a transformative influence in someone's journey out of a toxic relationship.

Sharing Knowledge and Awareness

The power of shared experiences, knowledge dissemination, and educational participation enhances the journey to recovery and personal growth after toxic relationships. Here's a deeper exploration of these vital aspects:

The Transformative Impact of Sharing Personal Experiences

The act of sharing personal stories about past relational challenges and the path to recovery serves as a beacon of hope and solidarity. It's a powerful way to validate and support others in similar situations. For instance, David's blog, where he candidly shared his journey, became a source of inspiration and encouragement for many. Similarly, Sarah's community talks on recognizing unhealthy patterns and establishing boundaries offer a valuable learning platform.

The shared stories of overcoming relationship challenges act as lighthouses in the fog of confusion and fear. Incorporate diverse testimonies, perhaps in a format like 'Voices of Resilience' where each story brings a unique perspective on overcoming adversity, adding depth and breadth to the concept of shared experiences.

Empowerment through Education and Awareness

Educational campaigns and initiatives are crucial in spreading awareness about the intricacies of challenging relationships and the path to healing. For example, Mark's webinars on emotional abuse awareness and recovery strategies have helped to enlighten and equip individuals with knowledge and tools. These efforts are not just about spreading information; they are about empowering people to recognize and navigate difficult dynamics confidently.

Nurturing Supportive Communities Through Knowledge Exchange

Creating environments for knowledge exchange, such as support group meetings or online forums, is essential in fostering a culture of openness and support. In these spaces, individuals like Jane can offer their expertise, such as legal advice, while others, like Daniel with his blog, provide a platform for expression and dialogue. These exchanges not only aid personal growth but also strengthen community ties, offering a nurturing space where individuals can share coping strategies, experiences, and insights.

These elements are not just standalone actions; they interweave to form a comprehensive support system. They empower individuals to navigate the aftermath of challenging relationships, providing them with tools for healing and growth. As we move through the journey of recovery, the emphasis is on using these strategies to create a supportive and knowledgeable environment that encourages healing and fosters personal development.

Providing Resources and Assistance

Providing information and resources for those recovering from toxic relationships is essential for support. Providing educational resources, as Sarah discovered through a book, can enlighten individuals about the dynamics of their situations, encouraging them to seek help. Directing people to specific resources, like John's discovery of a support group or Emma's use of a domestic abuse hotline, offers them structured support and immediate help. The empowerment derived from knowledge, as seen in James's exploration of a website detailing signs of emotional abuse, is invaluable in enabling informed decisions and seeking necessary help.

Connecting individuals to professional help plays a crucial role in their recovery. Therapy, as experienced by Sarah, offers expert guidance through the healing process, and understanding when to seek therapy, as John realized, is a critical step. The process of selecting the right therapist, as Mark did, ensures that the support provided aligns with the individual's specific needs. Therapy offers a confidential and safe space, as Maria found, to discuss concerns freely. Tailored therapeutic approaches, like those Paul encountered, provide personalized treatment, enhancing the healing journey.

Safety planning is essential for those in potentially dangerous situations, as illustrated by Lisa's strategy to protect herself and her children. Such planning should prioritize the individual's safety and well-being, incorporating measures like emergency contact lists, as in Mark's plan, and strategies for public safety, as James employed. Including emotional and psychological safety, as Emma did by integrating therapy and support groups, and addressing the needs of children, as Laura considered, are crucial aspects of a comprehensive safety plan. Recognizing the need for such planning, as seen in Michael's awareness, and executing it effectively, as Paul did, can provide a lifeline in times of crisis.

These elements work together to provide the support, knowledge, and means to navigate their recovery path, ensuring their safety and well-being, allowing them to pave the way for a future of healing and personal growth.

Emotional Support and Empowerment

Providing emotional support, fostering empowerment in decision-making, and nurturing self-care practices are pivotal. Emotional support, as illustrated by Sarah's journey, is a vital source of strength and validation. It involves more than just understanding the emotional impact of previous experiences; it's about being a constant source of support and empathy, much like what Lisa experienced from her friend. This support includes offering a safe space for open expression, actively listening, and providing encouragement and affirmation, which are crucial for rebuilding confidence and self-esteem. Emotional support also plays a key role in building resilience. Emma's support network was instrumental in helping her navigate challenges and celebrate her progress.

Empowering individuals in their decision-making process is equally important. This empowerment involves helping individuals reclaim control over their lives and rebuild self-confidence. It's about respecting their choices, even if it involves staying in challenging situations for a period, as Emily's friends showed. Providing non-judgmental support, active listening, and empowering small steps toward independence are essential components of this process. Offering resources and information, as done in David's case, equips individuals with the tools they need to make informed decisions. A safety net of support, celebration of independence, and acknowledgment of progress reinforces a sense of empowerment and autonomy.

Self-care is a cornerstone of emotional healing and recovery. Techniques like self-compassion and prioritizing well-being are also vital for emotional recovery. Self-care practices have a profound healing effect. Establishing a self-care routine that is tailored to individual needs, balancing self-care with daily responsibilities, recognizing signs of burnout, and emphasizing self-care during setbacks are crucial steps in the healing journey. Creating a supportive environment for self-care offers the resources and encouragement to maintain these practices.

Ultimately, these are not just supporting pillars in the recovery process; they are transformative forces. They help individuals not only in coping with the aftermath of past experiences but also in steering their journey towards sustained well-being and growth. These efforts contribute significantly to the overall health, resilience, and personal development of individuals navigating their path to recovery.

Creating Safe and Inclusive Spaces

Creating safe and inclusive spaces involves a multi-faceted approach that combines fostering supportive communities, promoting healthy boundaries, and celebrating diversity and resilience. How can we do it?

Fostering a Supportive Community

Supportive communities are essential in providing belonging and acceptance, crucial for healing. For instance, John found solace in an online support group, illustrating the power of such communities in offering connection and understanding. Safe spaces like these allow for open sharing and mutual support, as Sarah found in her local support group. Empathy and respect within these spaces, like Chris experienced in a community chat room, are foundational for creating nurturing environments. Diverse communities, as seen in Alex's experience, bring a range of perspectives and deepen the support available.

Promoting Healthy Boundaries

Maintaining healthy boundaries within these communities is essential for safety and respect. This involves setting clear communication guidelines and addressing disrespectful behavior effectively. Leaders in these communities, like David, play a pivotal role in modeling and reinforcing these boundaries. Open communication channels for reporting issues, conflict resolution techniques, and educating about the importance of boundaries are all crucial elements in maintaining a safe and respectful environment.

Celebrating Diversity and Resilience

Diversity in these communities enhances the richness of support and understanding. Varied recovery journeys, like those shared in a collection of personal stories, educate about different paths to healing. Cultural sensitivity workshops and diverse leadership ensure that various viewpoints inform community decisions. Collaborative projects and regular celebrations of members' journeys, such as an annual "Resilience Day," acknowledge the strength and resilience of individuals. Safe and inclusive language, along with a diverse range of recovery resources, ensures that healing is accessible to all.

In these spaces, emotional support and empowerment play significant roles. Techniques like active listening and validation, creating a non-judgmental space, and offering encouragement are integral to providing consistent support. Empowerment comes from helping individuals regain agency, build self-confidence, and respect their choices. Fostering a culture of self-care and healing through self-compassion, prioritizing well-being, and encouraging self-care practices during setbacks is vital.

These environments not only aid in the recovery and healing process but empowers individuals to reclaim their lives and embrace a future of well-being and growth.

Intervention and Safety

When approaching the critical subject of intervention and safety for individuals impacted by toxic relationships, it's essential to navigate with care, empathy, and an understanding of the complexities involved.

Staging an intervention begins with a thorough assessment of the situation to identify signs of abuse or distress. Consulting professionals is key to gaining insights for an effective approach. Creating a supportive team and planning the intervention carefully, including choosing the right setting and time, are vital steps. Using non-confrontational language and offering information and support are critical for a successful intervention. Listening actively, prioritizing safety, and respecting the individual's autonomy throughout the process are essential elements.

Safety and Emergency Plans

Post-intervention, assessing immediate safety is crucial. Discussing safe locations, compiling emergency contacts, and planning for the safety of children and pets are important steps. Helping to secure important documents and implementing security measures, like changing locks, enhances safety. Establishing a safety phrase or code, considering legal options like temporary restraining orders, and supporting mental health needs are vital components of a comprehensive safety plan. Introducing safety apps and technology, along with regular check-ins, ensures ongoing support and safety monitoring. Developing an emergency escape plan is also a critical element of safety planning.

Reporting Abuse

Reporting abuse carries both moral and legal obligations. Understanding the reporting process, including contacting relevant authorities, is crucial. Involving professionals in the process ensures expert handling of the situation. Legal protections are in place for those reporting abuse in good faith, with options for anonymous or confidential reporting. Collaborating with support services and providing documentation or witness testimony can strengthen the abuse case. Monitoring and follow-up with authorities ensures the case is handled appropriately, and that the victim receives necessary support. Engaging in community education and prevention efforts addresses the broader issue of abuse, while offering moral support to survivors is key to their recovery journey.

These require a delicate balance of empathy, proper planning, and respect for the individual's autonomy. Reporting abuse, while complex, is essential for protecting victims and ensuring their well-being. These efforts contribute significantly to the safety, recovery, and empowerment of individuals affected by toxic relationships.

Navigating Recovery and Thriving

The focus now needs to be on fostering a supportive environment and promoting personal growth and healthy relationships for individuals recovering from challenging experiences. A multifaceted approach is essential. This involves not only providing consistent support, but also empowering personal growth and fostering healthy relationships. Each element plays a crucial role in facilitating a holistic and sustainable journey toward healing and well-being.

Supporting Recovery with Empathy and Independence

Consistent emotional support is paramount in recovery. It's crucial to be a steady source of encouragement and understanding, actively listening and validating their experiences. This support, however, should be balanced by promoting independence, allowing individuals to take charge of their recovery at their own pace. Encouraging professional therapy or counseling and sharing informative resources can provide additional tools for healing. Emphasizing self-care practices and understanding that recovery is a non-linear process with potential setbacks are key aspects. Ensuring that support doesn't compromise your own safety or emotional health is also vital.

Empowering Personal Growth

Empowering individuals on their journey involves reinforcing their strengths and capabilities. Encourage them to engage in self-discovery, exploring their values, passions, and aspirations. Help set realistic personal development goals that are specific, measurable, achievable, relevant, and time bound. This process should include celebrating every achievement, big or small, to boost motivation and confidence. Provide consistent emotional support and resources that align with their personal growth goals. Be a role model in your commitment to personal growth, demonstrating by example the benefits of continuous self-improvement.

Nurturing Healthy Relationships

Assist in identifying characteristics of healthy relationships, such as mutual respect and trust. Encourage the pursuit of relationships that align with personal values and emotional well-being. Teach the importance of setting boundaries and effective communication skills within relationships. Emphasize empathy and mutual respect as foundations for nurturing balanced connections. Acknowledge and celebrate progress in forming healthier relationships, providing positive reinforcement for continued growth and balance.

Integrating Diverse Recovery Pathways

Recognize that recovery and thriving can take various forms. Encourage exploration of different methods and acknowledge that recovery is not a one-size-fits-all process. This can include community support, group therapy, and peer networks, providing a comprehensive support system.

Remember, your role as a supporter can be as simple as offering a listening ear, or as involved as guiding someone through safety planning and recovery. Each action, no matter how small, can be a pivotal point in someone's journey out of a challenging relationship. It's about creating spaces where stories can be shared without fear, where resources are accessible, and empowerment is not just a word, but a lived experience.

Let's carry forward the understanding that our actions, words, and presence can make a profound difference. Whether you're directly affected by toxic relationships or in a position to support someone who is, know that each step taken towards healing, every act of kindness, and every resource shared, contributes to a larger narrative of hope, resilience, and renewal.

Let's hold onto the belief that change is possible, healing is attainable, and a future filled with healthier relationships and deeper self-understanding is within reach.

Conclusion

As we close the pages of this journey, I want to take a moment to reflect on the path we've traversed together. This book wasn't just a collection of chapters; it was a shared expedition through the often-murky waters of toxic relationships. Each section was carefully crafted not only to enlighten but to empower and uplift you, the reader, who might be navigating these turbulent waters or helping someone who is.

The insights and strategies laid out in these pages are more than just words; they're tools and lifelines. We've dived deep into the essence of toxic relationships, unraveling their complex dynamics and the profound impact they can have. From recognizing early warning signs to cultivating resilience and empowerment, this book has been your guide and companion. Here are the key takeaways I want you to keep present:

1. **Understanding and awareness**: We've shone a light on the often-hidden facets of toxic relationships, offering clarity and understanding.

2. **Path to healing**: This book has charted a course for healing, blending self-reflection, mindfulness, and personal growth, tailored for every reader's unique journey.

3. **Empowerment and resilience**: The essence of bouncing back from adversity and reclaiming your power has been a cornerstone of our discussions.

4. **Community and compassion**: The book underscores the power of supportive networks, highlighting how communal strength can be a sanctuary for healing.

5. **Advocacy for change**: You've been encouraged to take a stand, to be part of a movement that challenges toxic norms and fosters healthier relationships.

To those of you who've walked through these chapters, feeling the weight of confusion, the erosion of self-esteem, or the struggle to break free, know that this book was written with you in mind. It's a testament to your resilience and a guide to reclaiming the joy and peace you deserve.

If these pages have resonated with you, I encourage you to share your experience in a review on Amazon. Your insights not only support my work as an author but also guide others who might be seeking their own path to healing. And for a space to continue this conversation and foster connections, I warmly invite you to join our Facebook community, where support and understanding are always within reach.

As you turn the last page, I want to reach out with a message of hope and solidarity. The journey to recovery is unique for each of us, filled with its own twists and turns. But remember, each step you take is a testament to your strength and a stride towards a future filled with light and positivity. You're not alone on this journey. My sincerest wish is for you to find peace, empowerment, and a renewed sense of self as you embrace the chapters of your life yet to be written. Here's to your journey towards a life filled with health, happiness, and relationships that uplift and fulfill you.

Bonus Chapter:

Taking Action Against Toxicity

At any given moment, you have the power to say, "This is not how the story is going to end." —Christine Mason Miller

Advocacy, in this context, is multifaceted and extends beyond individual support to encompass societal and systemic change.

It is not just about direct support for survivors. It involves a broader spectrum of activities, including raising public awareness, influencing policy and legal reforms, and fostering a supportive community network. This comprehensive approach ensures that we address the issue at both micro and macro levels.

Key to advocacy is raising awareness about the nature and implications of challenging relationships. This can be achieved through various initiatives such as social media campaigns, awareness events, and personal storytelling. These efforts educate the public, increase understanding, and challenge existing misconceptions. Moreover, conducting workshops and programs in different settings equips individuals with knowledge about identifying and avoiding toxic dynamics.

Another crucial aspect of advocacy is lobbying for legal and policy changes. This includes advocating for enhanced protections for survivors and holding individuals accountable for their actions. Efforts may also focus on lobbying for systemic changes such as mandated training for law enforcement and alterations in family court policies to better safeguard survivors and children.

Creating and nurturing support networks provides essential resources and safe spaces for survivors. These networks not only offer practical assistance but also foster a sense of solidarity and community among survivors. They serve as platforms for shared experiences and collective healing.

Advocates play a significant role in altering societal attitudes towards challenging relationships. Efforts are geared towards reducing stigma and promoting empathy and understanding. This cultural shift is crucial in creating an environment where survivors feel supported and validated.

Preventative measures are also a focus of advocacy. Educational initiatives aimed at empowering individuals with the knowledge and skills to recognize and steer clear of toxic dynamics are integral. These efforts contribute to reducing the recurrence of such relationships.

Ensuring that advocacy efforts are inclusive is also important. This means addressing the unique challenges and needs of diverse communities and individuals, ensuring that all voices are heard and catered to. Inclusive advocacy ensures that the needs of all affected individuals are considered, making the fight against toxic relationships a collective and far-reaching effort.

Reporting Abuse and Supporting Survivors

Recognizing and responding to abuse requires a keen awareness of its various manifestations. Vigilance in detecting signs of abuse across different settings is crucial, ensuring that timely and appropriate actions are taken. When abuse is identified, reporting it to relevant authorities, such as the police or child protective services, is a critical step towards ensuring the situation is addressed with the seriousness it warrants.

Supporting survivors extends beyond the act of reporting. It encompasses providing emotional support that is compassionate and non-judgmental. Such support validates their experiences and contributes significantly to their healing journey. It's about offering a safe haven where survivors feel understood and accepted, free from fear of judgment or stigma.

Guiding survivors towards comprehensive resources is a vital aspect of the support system. This includes connecting them to professional help, like therapy or counseling, which can address the deep-seated emotional impacts of abuse. Helping survivors develop safety plans for high-risk situations is an essential preventative measure. These plans should be carefully tailored to address immediate safety concerns and longer-term protective strategies.

Assisting survivors in navigating the legal system and involving legal authorities offers an added layer of protection and accountability. Creating safe spaces, both physical and emotional, where survivors can share their stories and receive support, is imperative in this process. Such environments foster a sense of community and solidarity, crucial for recovery.

Respect for the autonomy of survivors underpins all these efforts. While providing guidance and support, it's essential to acknowledge and respect their right to make their own decisions. This approach ensures that survivors feel empowered and in control of their journey towards healing and recovery.

In conclusion, tackling abuse and supporting survivors is a multi-faceted endeavor. It involves a combination of awareness, timely reporting, emotional support, resource provision, legal assistance, and respect for individual autonomy. Each element is critical in creating a supportive ecosystem that empowers survivors to heal and thrive post-abuse. This holistic approach paves the way for a future where survivors are not just safe, but are also thriving in an environment of understanding, respect, and empowerment.

Creating a Culture of Accountability

Creating a culture of accountability is a fundamental aspect in addressing toxic behaviors and fostering a healthy, respectful community. This process begins with a clear definition of accountability, which encompasses promoting honesty, responsibility, and the importance of making amends. It's essential for community settings to establish and communicate these behavioral standards clearly, ensuring everyone understands the expected conduct.

Education and awareness play a significant role in this cultural shift. Educating community members about the consequences of toxic behavior and the significance of being accountable is vital. It helps in fostering a deeper understanding of the impact of one's actions and the communal responsibility to uphold respect and integrity.

Open dialogue is encouraged, providing a platform for discussing actions, mistakes, and the willingness to make amends. Such conversations are crucial in maintaining transparency and fostering a sense of collective responsibility. To effectively manage conflicts and toxic behavior, structured conflict resolution procedures need to be implemented. These methods should focus not only on addressing the immediate issue but also on preventing recurrence.

Supporting individuals involves guiding them to understand the harm caused and assisting them in the process of repairing it.

Restorative justice practices are effective in repairing harm and fostering understanding between affected parties. These practices focus on healing rather than punishment, promoting reconciliation and mutual respect. Leadership within the community plays a critical role in modeling and promoting accountability. Leaders should embody the principles of responsibility and integrity, setting a positive example for the community.

Addressing harmful behavior promptly and fairly is crucial in maintaining community standards. It sends a clear message about the non-tolerance of toxic conduct. Alongside this, it's important to encourage self-reflection, helping individuals to introspect and identify areas for personal growth.

Finally, positive reinforcement of acts of accountability should be celebrated. Recognizing and applauding responsible behavior encourages a culture where accountability is valued and practiced by all.

Cultivating a culture of accountability involves a multifaceted approach that includes setting clear expectations, promoting open dialogue, implementing restorative practices, and supporting personal growth. Such an environment not only addresses harmful behavior but also fosters a community grounded in respect, understanding, and collective responsibility.

References

Allo Health. (2023, May 25). *How to build a healthy relationship after A toxic one.* Allo Health Care. https://www.allohealth.care/healthfeed/sex-education/healthy-relationship-after-a-toxic-one

A deeper look into gaslighting. (n.d.). The Hotline. https://www.thehotline.org/resources/a-deeper-look-into-gaslighting/

Admin. (2022, April 21). *9 tips on how to heal from A toxic relationship.* The Relationship Place. https://www.sdrelationshipplace.com/how-to-heal-from-a-toxic-relationship/

Allo Health. (2023, July 5). *Exploring the psychological impact of toxic relationships.* Allo Health Care. https://www.allohealth.care/healthfeed/sex-education/toxic-relationships-psychology

Assertive communication. (n.d.). Saprea. https://saprea.org/heal/approach/assertive-communication/

Assertiveness. (n.d.). San Diego State University. Retrieved November 27, 2023, from https://sacd.sdsu.edu/cps/self-care/presenting-concerns/assertiveness

Bajwa, F. (2021, July 26). *What to do when people in toxic relationships share.* The Shortform. https://medium.com/the-shortform/what-to-do-when-people-in-toxic-relationships-share-7d3750dcffb2

Bastos, F. (2023, October 14). *Overcoming boundary issues: A guide to healthy dynamics - mindowl.* Mindowl. https://mindowl.org/boundary-issues/

Brault, R. (n.d.). *A quote by Robert Brault.* Good Reads. Retrieved November 27, 2023, from https://www.goodreads.com/quotes/857668-life-becomes-easier-when-you-learn-to-accept-an-apology

Brown, V., Morgan, T., & Fralick, A. (2021). Isolation and mental health: Thinking outside the box. *General Psychiatry,* *34*(3), e100461. https://doi.org/10.1136/gpsych-2020-100461

Cacioppo, S., Grippo, A. J., London, S., Goossens, L., & Cacioppo, J. T. (2015). Loneliness: Clinical import and interventions. *Perspectives on Psychological Science, 10*(2), 238–249. https://doi.org/10.1177/1745691615570616

Charlie Health Editorial Team. (2023, April 28). *Toxic relationships & mental health.* Charlie Health. https://www.charliehealth.com/post/how-toxic-relationships-affect-your-mental-health

Cook, A. (2020, March 5). *How to forgive and move on in a relationship.* Dr. Alison Cook. https://www.dralisoncook.com/forgive-and-move-on-in-a-relationship/

Cooper-Lovett, D. C. (2018, November 28). *When and how to share your toxic relationship story.* A New Creation. https://www.anewcreationpsychotherapy.com/post/when-and-how-to-share-your-toxic-relationship-story

Cuncic, A. (2021, May 26). *What is radical acceptance?* Verywell Mind. https://www.verywellmind.com/what-is-radical-acceptance-5120614

Di Fabio, A., & Saklofske, D. H. (2020). The relationship of compassion and self-compassion with personality and emotional intelligence. *Personality and Individual Differences, 169,* 110109. https://doi.org/10.1016/j.paid.2020.110109

Ducharme, J. (2018, June 5). *How to tell if you're in a toxic relationship — and what to do about it.* Time. https://time.com/5274206/toxic-relationship-signs-help/

Emotional resilience. (2022, March 16). Wellbeing and Student Support. https://warwick.ac.uk/services/wss/topics/emotional_resilience/

Eric. (n.d.). *Tips on rebuilding and maintaining support after the isolation of abuse.* The Hotline. https://www.thehotline.org/resources/tips-on-rebuilding-and-maintaining-support-after-the-isolation-of-abuse/

Feuerman, M. (2021, April 5). *6 steps to leave a toxic relationship.* Verywell Mind. https://www.verywellmind.com/how-to-leave-a-toxic-marriage-4091900

Floyd, E. (2019, October 28). *Accepting reality using DBT skills.* Skyland Trail. https://www.skylandtrail.org/accepting-reality-using-dbt-skills/#:~:text=DBT%20Skill%3A%20Radical%20Acceptance&text=By%20embracing%20reality%20rather%20than

Forth, A., Sezlik, S., Lee, S., Ritchie, M., Logan, J., & Ellingwood, H. (2021). Toxic relationships: The experiences and effects of psychopathy in romantic relationships. *International Journal of Offender Therapy and Comparative Criminology*, *66*(15), 0306624X2110491. https://doi.org/10.1177/0306624x211049187

Gaba, S. (2021, March 12). *What is a toxic relationship?* Psychology Today. https://www.psychologytoday.com/us/blog/addiction-and-recovery/202103/what-is-toxic-relationship

Garwood, E. (2021, April 19). *I'm sorry you feel that way.* The University of Oklahoma Health Sciences Center. https://students.ouhsc.edu/Current-Students/Student-Wellbeing/Student-Wellness/Wellness-Articles/im-sorry-you-feel-that-wayunderstanding-gaslighting

Germer, C., & Neff, K. (2014). *Cultivating self-compassion in trauma survivors.* https://self-compassion.org/wp-content/uploads/2015/08/Germer.Neff_.Trauma.pdf

Gupta , S. (2023, July 18). *How compromise helps your relationship, according to a therapist.* Verywell Mind. https://www.verywellmind.com/compromise-in-relationships-7559559

Gupta, S. (2023, May 26). *How self-reflection can improve your mental health.* Verywell Mind. https://www.verywellmind.com/self-reflection-importance-benefits-and-strategies-7500858

Hardy, D.-A. (2023, June 27). *5 key strategies: Rebuild your life and thrive after toxic relationships and narcissistic abuse.* Inner Glow Revival. https://www.innerglowrevival.org/post/rebuild-and-thrive-after-toxic-relationships-and-narcissistic-abuse

Healthy relationship educators toolkit. (n.d.). https://www.loveisrespect.org/wp-content/uploads/2016/08/highschool-educators-toolkit.pdf

Healthy relationships. (n.d.). Center for Women and Families. https://www.thecenteronline.org/education/community-education/healthy-relationships/

Helping a friend in an unhealthy relationship or friendship. (n.d.). Mass. https://www.mass.gov/info-details/helping-a-friend-in-an-unhealthy-relationship-or-friendship

How to avoid toxic relationships and recover from them. (2023, July 10). Sabino Recovery. https://www.sabinorecovery.com/how-to-avoid-toxic-relationships-and-recover-from-them/

How to forgive — international forgiveness institute. (n.d.). International Forgiveness Institute. https://internationalforgiveness.com/need-to-forgive/

How to safely end an unhealthy relationship. (n.d.). The Jed Foundation. https://jedfoundation.org/resource/how-to-safely-end-unhealthy-relationships/

How we help. (2014, May 19). Break the Cycle. https://www.breakthecycle.org/how-we-help/

Lamoreux, K. (2021, July 22). *Just make it stop! 10 steps to end a toxic relationship.* Psych Central. https://psychcentral.com/blog/steps-to-end-a-toxic-relationship

Learn something series: Empathy, listening, & vulnerability. (n.d.). Human Resources. https://hr.princeton.edu/learn-something-series-empathy-listening-vulnerability

Mahler, J. (2023). Toxic relationship recovery. In *www.simonandschuster.com*. https://www.simonandschuster.com/books/Toxic-Relationship-Recovery/Jaime-Mahler/9781507220504

Martin, S. (2020, April 30). *How to set boundaries with toxic people.* Psych Central. https://psychcentral.com/blog/imperfect/2020/04/how-to-set-boundaries-with-toxic-people

Milstead, K. (2019, June 12). *Setting healthy boundaries after an abusive relationship.* Healthy Place. https://www.healthyplace.com/blogs/verbalabuseinrelationships/2019/6/setting-healthy-boundaries-after-an-abusive-relationship

Moore, C. (2019, June 2). *How to practice self-compassion: 8 techniques and tips.* Positive Psychology. https://positivepsychology.com/how-to-practice-self-compassion/

Nash, J. (2018, January 5). *How to set healthy boundaries & build positive relationships.* Positive Psychology. https://positivepsychology.com/great-self-care-setting-healthy-boundaries/

National Alliance on Mental Illness. (2020). *Pledge to be stigmafree.* Nami. https://www.nami.org/Get-Involved/Pledge-to-Be-StigmaFree

National Domestic Violence Hotline. (2018). *The national domestic violence hotline.* The National Domestic Violence Hotline. https://www.thehotline.org/

Need for closure. (n.d.). Arie Kruglanski. https://www.kruglanskiarie.com/need-for-closure

Northwestern University. (n.d.). *Healthy and Unhealthy Relationships: Center for Awareness, Response & Education.* Center for Awareness, Response and Education. https://www.northwestern.edu/care/get-info/relationship-violence/healthy-and-unhealthy-relationships.html

Pace, R. (2019, February 25). *How to save a toxic marriage: Dos and don'ts.* Marriage Advice. https://www.marriage.com/advice/save-your-marriage/can-a-toxic-marriage-ever-be-saved/

Parker, C. (n.d.). *A quote from I Can't Let Go.* GoodReads. https://www.goodreads.com/quotes/10113880-the-moment-you-start-to-wonder-if-you-deserve-better

Peer support workers for those in recovery. (2017, August 24). Samhsa. https://www.samhsa.gov/brss-tacs/recovery-support-tools/peers

Perry, E. (2023, March 23). *How to protect yourself from toxic empathy: 8 tips.* BetterUp. https://www.betterup.com/blog/how-to-protect-yourself-from-toxic-empathy

Rahman, I. (2022, August 26). *How to leave a toxic relationship.* Choosing Therapy. https://www.choosingtherapy.com/how-to-leave-a-toxic-relationship/

Ramsden, P. (2018, October 9). *The psychology of closure — and why some need it more than others.* The Conversation. https://theconversation.com/the-psychology-of-closure-and-why-some-need-it-more-than-others-104159

Rebuilding trust in yourself after a toxic relationship. (2023, August 25). ImPossible. https://www.impossiblepsychservices.com.sg/our-resources/articles/2023/08/25/rebuilding-trust-in-yourself-after-a-toxic-relationship

Recognizing the signs of unhealthy relationships. (n.d.). Mass.gov. https://www.mass.gov/info-details/recognizing-the-signs-of-unhealthy-relationships

Relationships. (n.d.). The University of Texas at El Paso. https://www.utep.edu/healthy-miner/resources/relationships.html

Resources for healthy relationships. (n.d.). Loyola Marymount University. Retrieved November 27, 2023, from https://studentaffairs.lmu.edu/wellness/lmucares/education/resourcesforhealthyrelationships/

Richer, L. (2021, October 8). *How to build mutual respect in your relationship.* Anchor Light Therapy Collective. https://anchorlighttherapy.com/how-to-build-mutual-respect-in-your-relationship/

Ripes, J. (2021, April 21). *13 tips for how to heal from a toxic relationship.* Modern Intimacy. https://www.modernintimacy.com/13-tips-for-how-to-heal-from-a-toxic-relationship/

Risk and protective factors for perpetration. (2021, November 2). Centers for Disease Control and Prevention. https://www.cdc.gov/violenceprevention/intimatepartnerviolence/riskprotectivefactors.html

Rogoza, R., Żemojtel-Piotrowska, M., Kwiatkowska, M. M., & Kwiatkowska, K. (2018). The bright, the dark, and the blue face of narcissism: The spectrum of narcissism in its relations to the metatraits of personality, self-esteem, and the nomological network of shyness, loneliness, and empathy. *Frontiers in Psychology, 9.* https://doi.org/10.3389/fpsyg.2018.00343

Rostorfer, C. (2017, November 28). *5 places you can find help you may not have known about.* One Love Foundation. https://www.joinonelove.org/learn/5-places-for-help-may-not-known/

Salters-Pedneault, K. (2022). *What you can do to help others feel validated.* Verywell Mind. https://www.verywellmind.com/what-is-emotional-validation-425336

Sarkis Ph.D, S. A. (2022, June 28). *How to recover from a toxic relationship.* Psychology Today. https://www.psychologytoday.com/us/blog/here-there-and-everywhere/202206/how-recover-toxic-relationship

Schultz, J. (2020, September 24). *Forgiveness in therapy: Help clients forgive themselves and others.* Positive Psychology. https://positivepsychology.com/forgiveness-in-therapy/

Segal, J., Robinson, L., & Smith, M. (2019, March 21). *Conflict resolution skills.* HelpGuide. https://www.helpguide.org/articles/relationships-communication/conflict-resolution-skills.htm

Sheri Heller, R. (2020, September 3). *The many faces of narcissism.* Invisible Illness. https://medium.com/invisible-illness/the-many-faces-of-narcissism-a7a1f65a5151

Silva Casabianca, S. (2014, January 4). *Signs your boundaries are being violated: Examples and how to deal.* Psych Central. https://psychcentral.com/relationships/signs-boundary-violations#:~:text=7%20Signs%20Someone%20Doesn

Souders, B. (2019, August 29). *24 forgiveness activities, exercises, tips and worksheets.* Positive Psychology. https://positivepsychology.com/forgiveness-exercises-tips-activities-worksheets/

Speak up about unhealthy relationships. (n.d.). That's Not Cool. https://thatsnotcool.com/speak-up-about-unhealthy-relationships/

Stine, M. (n.d.). *Toxic relationship awareness allows students to recognize harmful behaviors.* The Arrowhead. https://thearrowheadonline.com/731/features/toxicrelationshipawarenessallowsstudentstorecognizeharmfulbehaviors/

Support someone in an abusive relationship. (n.d.). The Hotline. https://www.thehotline.org/support-others/

Sutton, J. (2020, November 11). *10 best assertive communication worksheets and techniques.* Positive Psychology. https://positivepsychology.com/assertive-communication-worksheets/

Sutton, J. (2021a, May 1). *Cultivating reflection skills: 13 worksheets & journal templates.* Positive Psychology. https://positivepsychology.com/reflection-journal-worksheets/

Sutton, J. (2021b, November 9). *Conflict resolution in relationships and couples: 5 strategies.* Positive Psychology. https://positivepsychology.com/conflict-resolution-relationships/

Taitz, J. (2021, April 22). Radical acceptance can keep emotional pain from turning into suffering. *The New York Times.* https://www.nytimes.com/2021/04/22/well/mind/radical-acceptance-suffering.html

Telloian, C. (2021, September 15). *How many types of narcissism are there?* Psych Central. https://psychcentral.com/health/types-of-narcissism

Thakur, A. (2021, May 31). *Anand thakur quote.* Minimalist Quotes. https://minimalistquotes.com/anand-thakur-quote-64301/

Thakur, S. (2021, October 11). *150+ emotional quotes about an abusive relationship.* MomJunction. https://www.momjunction.com/articles/abusive-relationship-quotes_00776103/

Understanding and navigating toxic relationships: An expert's perspective. (n.d.). Integrative Psych. https://www.integrativepsych.nyc/resources/understanding-and-navigating-toxic-relationships-an-experts-perspective

Van Dyke, K. (2021, August 20). *How to emotionally detach from someone.* Psych Central. https://psychcentral.com/lib/the-what-why-when-and-how-of-detaching-from-loved-ones

VibewithAsia. (2023, September 24). *Strength in vulnerability: Revealing the pain of an abusive relationship.* Medium. https://medium.com/@vibewithasia/strength-in-vulnerability-revealing-the-pain-of-an-abusive-relationship-1fc6b3ae775d

Yadav, A. (2023, March 16). *Toxic relationships and burnout in leadership: How to protect yourself and your team*. XMonks. https://xmonks.com/toxic-relationships-and-burnout-in-leadership-how-to-protect-yourself-and-your-team/

Made in the USA
Middletown, DE
13 January 2024

47805345R00096